on track shorts ...

Iggy And The Stooges

every album, every song

Robert Day-Webb

sonicbondpublishing.com

Sonicbond Publishing Limited
www.sonicbondpublishing.co.uk
Email: info@sonicbondpublishing.co.uk

First Published in the United Kingdom 2025
First Published in the United States 2025

British Library Cataloguing in Publication Data:
A Catalogue record for this book is available from the British Library

Copyright Robert Day-Webb 2025

ISBN 978-1-78952-360-7

The right of Robert Day-Webb to be identified
as the author of this work has been asserted by him
in accordance with the Copyright, Designs and Patents Act 1988.
All rights reserved. No part of this publication may be reproduced, stored in a
retrieval system or transmitted in any form or by any means, electronic, mechanical,
photocopying, recording or otherwise, without prior permission in writing from
Sonicbond Publishing Limited

Typeset in ITC Garamond Std & ITC Avant Garde Gothic
Printed and bound in England

Graphic design and typesetting: Full Moon Media

Acknowledgements

I would like to dedicate this book, with love, to my family:
Rie, Josh, Lolly, Matt and Dan.

I would also like to say a big thank you to Stephen Lambe for allowing me the opportunity to write another book for Sonicbond Publishing.

Huge thanks also go to all the people who have previously carried out the invaluable research utilised in this book.

Finally, of course, the biggest thank you of all goes out to Iggy, Ron, Scott, Dave, James, and indeed, everyone else who has passed through the ranks of The Stooges for all the memorable and influential music you created ... *Raw Power* indeed!

on track shorts ...

Iggy And The Stooges

Contents

Introduction 7
Prologue 9
The Stooges (1969) 15
Fun House (1970) 23
Raw Power (1973) 33
Post-Break-Up/Reunion 47
The Weirdness (2007) 52
Ready To Die (2013) 58
Further Related And Recommended Albums And Songs 64
Epilogue 72
Bibliography 74

Introduction

Exploding onto the late 1960s scene against a backdrop of generational and racial tensions, the Vietnam War and hippy idealism, The Stooges were a band unlike any other before. A bunch of misfit Mid-Western delinquents, their frontman, James Osterberg (later christened Iggy Stooge, then Iggy Pop), was a performer extraordinaire. He was confrontational and theatrical and practically invented the stage dive. He was also not averse to smearing himself in peanut butter or raw meat and cutting himself with broken glass on stage! This maniacal entertainer was originally joined by the Asheton brothers, Ron and Scott, and their pal, Dave Alexander. Ron, lead guitarist, delivered loud and memorable, albeit simplistic and minimalist, riffs covered in distortion, whilst Scott and Dave provided a primitive rhythm section groove of finesse-free noise.

This original lineup delivered a debut album (*The Stooges*) of primal and brutal-sounding riffs and drones, played with economic efficiency and limited technical proficiency. The record, ironically released around the time of the Woodstock Festival, fused blues, psychedelia and garage rock but went unheralded at the time and flopped. Undeterred, the band were determined to follow their own musical course and proceeded to release a more sophisticated sophomore effort (*Fun House*), which took their signature primitive rock noise and audaciously added sprinkles of free jazz into the mix. However, this album again flopped, after which the band began to fracture. Several personnel changes ensued, but by the spring of 1971, it was pretty much all over, with the band having been dropped by its record label and various band members in the throes of drug addiction.

However, the story did not end there. Later in 1971, Iggy fortuitously crossed paths with a certain Mr. David Bowie, who just so happened to be a big fan of Iggy's. This union ultimately led to a creative rebirth for Iggy and the band. With a new, swaggering lead guitarist in place, one James Williamson, and the Asheton brothers making up the new rhythm section, the reconstituted (and slightly re-named) Iggy and The Stooges ended up delivering a third album (*Raw Power*) of nihilistic ferocity. Once again, however, the album bombed, leaving the band to limp on playing deteriorating live shows until early 1974. It was at this juncture that the band decided to call it a day. After several years of flop albums, poor reviews and no money, and with various band members physically and mentally spent and drug-addled, that was the end of the Stooges story for nearly 30 years.

Iggy went on to reconnect with David Bowie and managed to resurrect his career, ultimately enjoying a sustained solo music career. Indeed, with a sideline in acting and against all the odds, Iggy subsequently went on to become a mainstream pop culture icon.

The Asheton's, meanwhile, also continued to pursue their own respective musical projects. James Williamson, on the other hand, eventually left the music business and went on to enjoy a successful career in the electronics industry.

However, once again, this is not the end of the story. 2003 saw the surprise reunion of the original lineup (barring Dave Alexander, who had sadly passed away in 1975), with Iggy, Ron and Scott playing together again under The Stooges banner. The band toured extensively and performed to rapturous crowds across the globe, belatedly being treated like conquering heroes. Finally, they achieved the respect and adulation that had been sorely lacking the first time around. There was even a new album in 2007 (*The Weirdness*). Sadly, 2009 saw the untimely death of Ron Asheton, although this did not bring an end to the band's tale. The subsequent return of guitarist James Williamson to the fold shortly after Ron's death also saw the return of the Iggy and The Stooges moniker.

The band were finally inducted into the Rock and Roll Hall of Fame in 2010 and the Williamson lineup also released a new album in 2013 (*Ready To Die*). However, more sad news ensued in 2014 when drummer Scott Asheton passed away. This ultimately led to the cessation of the band.

Although a rather sad end to the story, the enduring legacy of this band cannot be overstated. A band unlike any other that had come before, The Stooges' music and image have influenced countless other bands and artists that have subsequently followed in their wake. The band's first three seminal albums, essentially odes to the disillusioned and disaffected youth of the world, pre-empted and heavily influenced several music genres that followed – punk rock, noise rock, alternative rock, grunge rock and even heavy metal.

Too weird, freaky and dangerous for mainstream acceptance back in the day, after their 1974 break-up, the band's legacy and influence grew over the ensuing decades, thus ensuring their everlasting and prominent placing in the annals of rock 'n' roll history.

Raw, intense, ferocious, full of attitude, and yes, vulgar, they were quite possibly the most dangerous rock 'n' roll band of all time!

Prologue

Iggy Pop was born James Newell Osterberg Jr. on 21 April 1947 in Muskegon, Michigan, and was raised in a trailer park in Ypsilanti, just outside the university town of Ann Arbor, Michigan. (Against this lower-middle-class background setting, the 'trailer trash' insults he endured as a kid actually helped Iggy in the long run, making him extremely competitive and instilling that thirst for success, etc.) The young Osterberg was apparently around nine years of age when he first became fascinated by the sound of 'industrial hum'. Indeed, any kind of machinery and its sound fascinated the young boy, so it was no surprise then when the youngster began playing drums at school. Subsequently, at age 14, the young Osterberg got his first drum kit when his interest in music was well and truly sparked in the early 1960s by the sounds of Duane Eddy, Ray Charles and Chuck Berry. In 1962, the young Osterberg initiated his own musical endeavour when he formed a musical duo with a school friend, The Megaton Two, in which he, of course, played the drums. This duo later expanded into the group The Iguanas circa 1964. Over the course of the next year or two, The Iguanas subsequently became a very popular local rock 'n' roll band, playing gigs at local high schools and frat parties at the University of Michigan, where they specialised in the à la mode British Invasion sounds of the day (including lots of Beatles tunes).

In July 1965, Osterberg graduated from high school and carried on playing with The Iguanas, who, by this time, were now playing clubs and periodically backing visiting musicians like The Shangri-Las. The band also managed to release a single, a cover of Bo Diddley's 'Mona'. In September 1965, Osterberg enrolled at the University of Michigan to study anthropology but dropped out after only one term. In November 1965, he decided to quit The Iguanas and instead joined local blues band The Prime Movers. It was around this time that the young Osterberg acquired the nickname 'Iggy', a slightly derisory sobriquet courtesy of his new bandmates, who couldn't resist a little dig at Osterberg's previous band.

Around the autumn of 1966, now aged 19, Iggy decided to quit not only The Prime Movers but also the entire Ann Arbor area, feeling that he had squeezed everything he could out of Ann Arbor. He, therefore, embarked on a trip of discovery to Chicago, whereupon he set about investigating the blues by hanging out and playing with some real authentic bluesmen. Iggy subsequently learned a lot during his brief time there and, upon his return to Ann Arbor, was determined to utilise his recent Chicago experience to help birth his own truly original music aspirations. He now knew that he no longer wanted to be a drummer, and he also realised that he was not destined to be a true blues player either, but he had been instilled with an urge to form his own band and a desire to create something entirely new, original and unique. He now just needed to find some like-minded guys…

Ron Asheton was born on 17 July 1948 in Washington DC and moved to Ann Arbor late in 1963 (after the passing of his father) with the rest of his family, including slightly younger brother Scott (born on 16 August 1949). Ron's musical ambitions started early when, at the age of five, he had taken accordion lessons. Later, at the age of ten, he started guitar lessons. The youngster's musical interests subsequently waned a little, but the likes of Bob Dylan, The Beatles and The Yardbirds later reignited his interest in guitar playing. At this time, he developed a minimal playing style based on three-chord simplicity. Brother Scott also knew from an early age that he wanted to be involved in the music biz. He was around ten years old when he fell in love with the radio and listening to music. Since his older brother had snagged the guitar, Scott decided to pursue the drums and subsequently started by playing the snare drum at school. At around 14 years old, he started borrowing drum sets from other guys as he could not afford one.

At some point, Scott became good friends with another local lad, Dave Alexander (born 3 June 1947), although Dave later gravitated more naturally to older brother Ron because of their shared love of British rock music. So much so that, around mid-1965, both Dave and Ron ended up selling their motorcycles in order to fund a visit to England, with Ron ditching school. They rather naively thought that they would see the likes of The Beatles and The Stones simply wandering around the streets! Obviously, this did not happen, but they did end up meeting local bands (in London and Liverpool) and also got to see the likes of The Who in concert. They were only there for about a month before they returned to Ann Arbor. Ron attempted to go back to school, but he just could not cope since his mind was now well and truly set on a career playing music.

Ron attempted to form a band with his brother Scott, Dave Alexander and another local lad, Bill Cheatham. This project was entitled The Dirty Shames, but it was more of a conceptual band than an actual functioning band – they did not really play at all, but they apparently looked very cool! Ron also briefly played in The Prime Movers, where he crossed paths with their drummer, a certain Mr. 'Iggy' Osterberg. However, Ron's tenure as an actual player in this band was very short due to his limited bass-playing ability at that time! Ron then subsequently played with The Chosen Few as their bassist. Interestingly, future Stooge James Williamson had been a founding member of The Chosen Few (circa the mid-1960s), although his tenure in the band was brief. Some sources say there was a slight membership overlap with Ron despite James saying not (insisting that he met both Iggy and Ron slightly later in 1966).

It was actually after Ron's trip to England that he first became acquainted with Iggy (whilst Iggy was still with The Iguanas). Iggy has often mentioned in interviews that he first became aware of Ron, Scott and Dave when they used to hang around outside the record store (Discount Records) he used to work at in Ann Arbor in the mid-1960s (where he supplemented his respective Iguanas and Prime Movers income). However, Iggy and Ron's paths crossed musically around this time, too, given their shared Prime Movers membership. Regardless of when they actually first met, the relationship between Ron and Iggy developed steadily into a real friendship over time, and at some point around this juncture, Iggy also became a drum mentor to Ron's aspiring drummer brother, Scott.

So, when Iggy returned from his Chicago expedition, he knew exactly who to call on ... and so it was that, in 1967, Ron, Scott and Dave eventually hooked up with Iggy to form a band, all of them with a like-minded quest to create something truly new and original. Initially, they spent a lot of time listening to music and chatting about music – whilst the entire band were keen on artists such as The Velvet Underground, The Rolling Stones and John Lee Hooker, Dave was also a Love fan, whilst Ron was also inspired by the likes of Jimi Hendrix, The Pretty Things and Pete Townshend. Iggy was keen on The Doors and Van Morrison but also more avant-garde stuff, like Harry Partch and John Cage, which he had been exposed to back in Ann Arbor. Other left-field influences on the band at this early stage also included the likes of Ravi Shankar and Gregorian chants.

Ultimately, the band decided that their strategy would be to ignore more conventional music form and structure. However, there were several months where nothing much actually happened, as confirmed by Iggy himself (in his 1982 biography, *I Need More*):

We formed a band and did nothing but talk bullshit for months and months. I actually provoked the fellows into practising by, mainly, scoring a quantity of grass or hash – I was very serious about rehearsal. I was very ambitious, you know. I never wanted to be anything but at the top, the most noticed or the most famous ... But these were the laziest juvenile delinquent sort of pig snobs ever born. Really spoiled rotten and babied by their mothers.

Indeed, early rehearsals (at the Asheton family house) were sorely lacking in motivation, and Iggy found himself having to dangle the cannabis carrot in front of his bandmates to solicit some work from them! Fuelled by marijuana and LSD and with a wide variety of musical influences floating around them, the band were eventually inspired to create some unique and experimental music. Heavily improvised and rather primitive in nature (the band members were barely technically proficient musicians at this early stage), the free-form music also incorporated a fair number of unusual homemade instruments (the band did not really have any proper songs, rather just improvised jams incorporating various sound effects plus a few riffs, with Iggy grunting over the music!). According to Ron Asheton, they started out with Iggy getting a Farfisa organ (before slightly later moving on to Hawaiian guitar), with Scott using timbales, a snare drum and oil drums. Ron would use the bass guitar with a fuzz tone and a wah-wah pedal. The homemade instrumental inventions/experiments included putting a mic against the lip of a blender with water in it, Iggy dancing on a washboard (and/or sheet metal) with spiked golf shoes on, the use of a mic and funnel/cone to help create weird feedback sounds and a vacuum cleaner was also apparently incorporated into things in some way! Initially, it was Dave who used to operate all the bizarre instrumentation whilst Iggy played his keyboards, Ron played his bass and Scott played his makeshift drum set.

Rehearsals shifted to Dave's house for a while before the band finally moved into a house together to facilitate easier and more convenient rehearsals. (The band would eventually reside in a succession of band houses, and sometime later, in 1968, the band moved into the notorious 'Fun House', aka 'Stooge Manor', aka 'Stooge Hall'.)

Regarding the band's eventual choice of name, it was Ron Asheton who was responsible for this. Ron really liked the famous comedy trio The Three Stooges and likened the band to them. The band's use of acid at the time then lent them the 'Psychedelic' tag. Ron (taken from the 2005 *The Stooges* CD reissue liner notes):

> We dropped acid and were sitting around trying to think of a band name. Just as I was getting off, it hit me: How about The Stooges? Because we're like The Three Stooges ... And we're on acid ... The Psychedelic Stooges! That's it!

Ron even went as far as to check with original Stooge Moe Howard that it was okay to use the name – and, thankfully, it was.

A guy called Ron Richardson briefly became their first manager, and the band finally made their live debut at a private party held at Richardson's house on Halloween (1967), whereupon they delivered a short set of improvised instrumental rock 'n' roll fused with avant-garde sounds. Iggy, apparently dressed in a Victorian nightdress and adorned with an aluminium foil wig for the occasion, played Hawaiian guitar whilst Scott hammered away on oil drums. Ron, meanwhile, played bass guitar, making full use of a fuzz box and wah-wah effects, leaving Dave to twiddle the amp dials, etc.

Not long after the gig, the band decided that they needed a more conventionally structured lineup, resulting in Iggy as the designated frontman, Ron as lead guitarist, Dave on bass and Scott on drums.

The band's first proper public show (and as a functioning quartet) followed in January 1968 at Detroit's Grande Ballroom before a second gig in March at the same venue. Audiences were bemused, repulsed and even scared but were ultimately transfixed by what they witnessed! By the band's second gig, Iggy had moved on from the Victorian nightdress and foil wig to the now familiar shirtless/tight jeans look (apparently, Iggy got the idea of performing shirtless from a book on Egyptology, where he had noted that the Pharaohs never wore shirts and looked very cool!), but he was, however, still also sporting white face make-up and a perm (the white face and perm would last a few more gigs before being ditched)! Scott was still also playing oil drums and the band were still delivering 20-minute-length sets of free-form, feedback-laden improvised music adorned with wah-wah effects and droning bass sounds. Vocally, Iggy was emitting a mixture of almost scat-like vocals and primal howls. (The oddball homemade instruments period did not actually last too long in reality – just the early rehearsals and the Halloween party, really. By April 1968, the band were mainly using traditional instrumentation.)

Incidentally, a newspaper review of their second professional gig referred to the frontman as 'Iggy' Osterberg, whereupon Iggy decided to keep it as his stage name.

It was at these very early shows that Iggy developed his controversial frontman persona, bewildering and mesmerising audiences at the same time. Iggy took inspiration from the likes of Mick Jagger and Jim Morrison but twisted it into his own unique thing (Iggy had actually witnessed The Doors live in October 1967 and had been impressed by Jim Morrison's frontman act).

Despite terrifying audiences in the Michigan area with their weird and wild antics, the band slowly but surely developed a small but devoted fanbase as they gigged relentlessly over the ensuing year (and they essentially became the Grande Ballroom's house band for a while over that first year or so, supporting lots of visiting big bands – the likes of Cream, The Mothers of Invention, Sly and the Family Stone, Blood, Sweat & Tears, etc.). Throughout 1968, the band also started to play in smaller club venues where Iggy practically invented the stage dive, jumping into audiences and confronting them. Indecent exposures also started to occur!

Around the spring of 1968, one Jimmy Silver (a friend of MC5 manager John Sinclair) became the band's manager. Jimmy subsequently helped the band move into the MC5's circle, and over the course of 1968, the Stooges essentially became protégés of the fellow Michigan-based band, which ultimately proved very beneficial to their career. Indeed, they played a lot with the MC5 during 1968 and became affectionately known as the MC5's 'little brother' band.

The Detroit area actually boasted a thriving rock 'n' roll scene at the time (the likes of the MC5, Bob Seger, Ted Nugent, Alice Cooper, etc.), but the musically limited and primitive-sounding Psychedelic Stooges were not exactly the most likely to be signed to a major record label!

However, in September 1968, one Danny Fields (Elektra's Head of Promotions/Publicity Director) flew to Detroit to check out the MC5 with a view to signing them to the label (Elektra had hit the big time the previous year with The Doors and was looking to expand its roster of artists). Fields was impressed by the MC5 but was subsequently encouraged (by John Sinclair and MC5 guitarist Wayne Kramer) to also check out their little brother band. Fields did indeed check out the Stooges and was blown away by what he witnessed. Danny Fields (taken from the 2005 *The Stooges* CD reissue liner notes):

When I saw The Stooges, it was love at first sight. Even more than Iggy as a performer, which would have been stunning enough, it was the sound of the band ... with The Stooges, you went sailing right over the cliff of modern musical taste into places you'd never been before. Art, to me, was something I couldn't imagine in my mind, and that's what The Psychedelic Stooges showed me. It was like they were making the music I'd waited my whole life to hear.

Danny subsequently called up Jac Holzman (Elektra's President) and said he wanted to sign not only the MC5 but also The Stooges. Fields then returned to New York and convinced Holzman to sign them both (after discussions with both group's respective managers, John Sinclair and Jimmy Silver). A celebratory signing gig with both bands subsequently took place on 8 October 1968 (the actual date of the contract) with Jac Holzman and Bill Harvey (Elektra's Vice President) in attendance. On the contract, the band were simply named The Stooges, the 'Psychedelic' part having just been dropped.

The Stooges (1969)

Personnel:
Iggy Pop: vocals (credited as 'Iggy Stooge')
Ron Asheton: guitar
Dave Alexander: bass
Scott Asheton: drums
Additional musicians:
John Cale: viola on 'We Will Fall'
Recorded at The Hit Factory, New York (April 1969)
Produced by John Cale
UK release date: September 1969
US release date: August 1969
Chart places: UK: did not chart, US: 106

Post-signing, the band fulfilled live dates until February 1969. The band then readied themselves for the forthcoming debut album recording sessions. Once signed, the band soon realised that they needed to come up with some properly structured songs (rather than freak-out improv jams – early 'songs' had included the likes of 'Asthma Attack', 'I'm Sick', 'Goodbye Bozos' and 'The Dance Of Romance' (aka 'Dance Of The Romance', 'Dance And Romance')) to record for their debut LP. Ron Asheton promptly stepped up to the plate and came up with two killer riffs that formed the basis of future classics-in-waiting 'I Wanna Be Your Dog' and 'No Fun'. In addition, the band also composed two other songs in preparation for the album recording sessions – '1969' and 'Ann' (indeed, the songwriting modus operandi at this time was that Iggy would generally help mould Ron's initial riffs into fully fledged songs and would come up with some lyrics, too). Armed with these four solid tunes, the band headed to New York to start recording.

Recording took place at the Hit Factory studios and legend has it that the sessions apparently began on April Fool's Day! The band's original strategy had been to take the four songs they had, record the structured 'proper song' part, which would be of standard song length, and then extend the running time of each of the songs by several minutes by adding some improvised music. In addition to these four numbers, they also worked up a couple of other improvised pieces. Dave had suggested an Indian-sounding chant as the basis for another number (which became 'We Will Fall') whilst the band also worked up a studio version of their live staple, 'Asthma Attack'. Not surprisingly, when these extended tracks were presented to Elektra, the record company had none of it and insisted that the band needed more songs. The band lied through their teeth and said that this was not a problem! Legend has it that the band quickly returned to the Chelsea Hotel, where they were staying in New York, and wrote another three songs over the next 24 hours. An additional recording session was set up to record the new songs ('Real Cool Time', 'Not Right' and 'Little Doll').

Ex-Velvet Underground member John Cale had been chosen to produce the record, having just worked with Nico on her *The Marble Index* album. The band were more than happy with this decision since they were fans of The Velvet Underground. Cale would apparently appear at the sessions wearing a Dracula cape and was also soon joined by his friend Nico, who would apparently sit at his side knitting (Iggy and Nico would also indulge in a brief liaison for about a month or so around this time)! All went well in the studio until the mixing stage. For some reason, Cale's original mixes were deemed unacceptable, some complaints being that they were either too over-thought or too arty and not a true representation of the band's sound. A lot of sources state that Jac Holzman and Iggy then went in and remixed the album, but it appears that the truth is that a guy called Lewis Merenstein was called in to do the final remix (he had just recently produced Van Morrison's *Astral Weeks* LP).

The LP was eventually released in the US in August, around the time of the Woodstock festival (ironic, given that the album's nihilistic and primitive music was the complete antithesis of that festival's peace 'n' love hippy vibe!). The album appeared with a cover that aped The Doors' debut LP cover (with a focus on the band members' faces), which was probably Elektra's idea since that band was also on their label. Iggy was also credited as 'Iggy Stooge' on the album sleeve, which Iggy was apparently not too happy about. This was clearly Elektra's decision as, in reality, Iggy had started using 'Pop' as his surname by the end of 1968 (he had chosen this name in honour of an old Ann Arbor acquaintance called Jim Popp). However, the music media, in general, would continue to refer to him as Iggy Stooge up until at least 1972. (Incidentally, Scott Asheton also acquired his nickname, 'Rock Action', around this time, too.)

Upon release, the LP met with some critical acclaim, but the lack of proper support from Elektra ensured that the record was a bit of a commercial failure nationally (it did receive moderate radio airplay in the Detroit area but not on a national scale). The album ended up selling about 32,000 copies during its first year and peaked at a lowly number 106 on the US album charts.

Rolling Stone called the record 'loud, boring, tasteless, unimaginative and childish' in its October 1969 review of the album! High praise indeed, although the reviewer in question did actually go on to concede that, regardless of his assessment of the record, he still kind of liked it!

Creem, meanwhile, proved to be a big supporter of the band and, in their August 1969 review, had the good foresight to highlight Ron's contribution to the make-up of the album:

Throughout the album, [Ron] Asheton reveals himself as an insane master of the power the Stooges channel into their music. This is probably the guitar style of the future.

Other press quotes on the debut album came from *Cash Box* ('The Stooges, because of the intensity of their passion and the integrity of their musicianship, are at any volume hard and hot'), *Record World* ('The Stooges are a hot new group, and understandably so after hearing this collection of definitive hard rock') and *Billboard* ('A rough and raw Rolling Stones-type sound that glitters with the addition of strong lyric content and sophisticated pop execution').

Brutal and primal, minimalist and simplistic, it proved to be a record both ahead of its time and out of time. Simple three-chord riffs, delivered via feedback-laden and wah-wah distortion, combine with correspondingly simple but equally effective lyrics (reflecting Iggy's cynical take on the boredom of life in Ann Arbor at the time), delivered by Iggy's snarling, growling and crooning vocals. All of this is backed up forcefully by the incredibly loud rhythm section of Scott and Dave, whose simplistic and barely proficient abilities actually lend themselves to the primitive rock 'n' roll sounds on the record. Technically speaking, the songwriting is basic and the musicianship on display is hardly accomplished, but it does proffer listeners with an unsophisticated take on the blues and psychedelia that was unlike anything else that had come before it and it is understandable why some see this as a landmark proto-punk album. Understandably, the album has also consistently made it onto *Rolling Stone*'s '500 Greatest Albums Of All Time' lists.

The limited lyrical content on the album was actually very deliberate on Iggy's behalf, too. Iggy had loved kids' TV host Soupy Sales as a child and remembered that Soupy would tell kids to write letters to the show but keep them to 25 words or less. Iggy subsequently used this philosophy on the LP, recognising that he was no Bob Dylan! 'There must not be more than 100 words on that album,' Iggy told an interviewer in 1983, 'so I made each one count.' (Taken from the 2005 *The Stooges* CD reissue liner notes.)

However, with its more structured songwriting, the album probably did not reflect the true sound of the band at that time. Scott Asheton later complained to *Classic Rock*:

> They told us that we couldn't do an album the way the band were live. The band weren't anything like what came up on the first album. We didn't sound like that, we didn't play like that and they wanted to get us on an album, but they told us we had to write songs, and so we came up with those little drippy, dweepy little songs that were on the first album. When I hear it, it sounds like a different band. Like I say, that album was not us.

After the recording of the album, the band returned to Ann Arbor and continued touring extensively (for the rest of the year), with Iggy, in particular, raising the stakes with regards to his wild and unpredictable live performances.

This album has been reissued many times over the years, but particular reissues of note include the following: a two-disc CD release (on Elektra/Rhino) with bonus tracks (including some original John Cale mixes, alternate vocal versions and 'full' versions) in 2005; Elektra/Rhino Handmade issued the Collectors' Edition in 2010, an expanded two-disc CD set (with the 2005 bonus tracks being built upon including further Cale mixes as well as some alternate takes, etc.) with an additional 7" vinyl containing 'Asthma Attack Pt. 1' and 'Asthma Attack Pt. 2'; 2019 saw the digital release (Elektra/Rhino again) of the 50th Anniversary Deluxe Edition which featured a remaster of the original album, a remaster of the John Cale mix of the album (the Cale mixes finally being mastered at their correctly intended speed – previously, their bonus track appearances had been mastered at a slower speed than intended) and the same bonus tracks as on the 2010 Collectors' Edition.

'1969' (The Stooges)

Opening with some brief, funky wah-wah guitar sounds accompanied by some military-style drum beats, Iggy commences proceedings with a 'Well, alright' before the tempo really kicks into gear. Prominent and characterful handclaps back the instrumentation throughout whilst Ron's driving two-chord riff propels the song ever forward. Scott and Dave's rhythm section groove, meanwhile, provides the glue that holds the whole thing together. Ron continues to impress throughout with his fuzzy and distorted lead guitar work, which gets more intricate as the song progresses. Iggy, vocally, also shines, sneering and snarling away with punky snottiness.

The song's rhythm essentially borrows from Bo Diddley, but the band twist and mould it into their own idiosyncratic groove. This track makes for a great album opener, and it is no surprise that *Rolling Stone* magazine listed it number 35 on its 100 Greatest Guitar Songs Of All Time list. Interestingly (and perhaps somewhat surprisingly), according to the band, Ron's legendary riff idea stemmed from a small musical section in The Byrds' 'Tribal Gathering' (from their *The Notorious Byrd Brothers* album). The lyrical content of the song, meanwhile, pertains to Iggy's personal feelings towards life in 1969, and as *Creem* magazine so succinctly put it, this track is 'the perfect expression of the oldest complaint of rebellious anarcho/crazy youth.'

The song was also released as a single in France, backed with fellow album track 'Real Cool Time'.

'I Wanna Be Your Dog' (The Stooges)

Heavy, distorted guitar kickstarts this next number before Ron's distinctive riff (which gave birth to the entire song) starts up and takes hold. The rock instrumentation is then soon accompanied by the characteristic sound of jingling sleigh bells (courtesy of producer John Cale, who also provides his piano skills on this one). Iggy's drawling vocals then kick in as he proceeds to deliver a rather dark lyric about submission, degradation and self-humiliation.

This menacing tune, although musically simplistic, continues apace and pummels the listener into submission with its relentless three-minute aural attack. Ron eventually brings the song to a close with a nicely distorted guitar solo. Interestingly, Iggy has stated (on record) that the chords in this song are basically the same as the ones in Jimi Hendrix's 'Highway Chile' but done Ron-style with overtones of The Who and The Velvet Underground! If one listens to both tracks, this claim does indeed sound feasible, albeit with Ron delivering them in a far heavier, distorted and droning fashion.

Creem magazine described the track, arguably the band's signature song, as 'reminiscent of early Velvet Underground music, carrying it into even more bizarre levels.' This song also consistently makes it onto *Rolling Stone* magazine's list of '500 Greatest Songs Of All Time'.

The track was released as a single in the US in July 1969 backed with fellow album track '1969' (and was also released in Canada and Australia with the same B-side). It was released in Italy as a single backed with a different album track, 'Ann'.

The mono single version of the track was included as a bonus track on the 2010 Collectors' Edition reissue of the album.

'We Will Fall' (The Stooges)
Listeners are now treated to a real change of pace and style here with this chant-based drone. It is very Velvet Underground-esque at times due to producer John Cale's distinctive droning viola work throughout. Slow handclap accompaniment to the sombre instrumentation throughout also adds further flavour to this highly atmospheric piece. Iggy sings of waiting for Nico to show up for a tryst at the Chelsea Hotel over the chanting band whilst subtle but effective lead guitar sounds from Ron permeate the background, adding a slightly spooky vibe to proceedings. It is an incredibly hypnotic and compelling piece based on an original (Eastern/Indian-like chant/drone) idea brought in by bassist Dave Alexander.

Iggy's rather sombre-sounding vocals conclude with a repetitious 'Goodbye' before the instrumentation – dominated by Cale's viola and Ron's funky wah-wah guitar – leads the song to a slightly overdue conclusion (the track is just over ten minutes long). It is a bit of a Marmite song, with some fans loving it while others cannot stand it, stating that it is nothing but an overlong, boring, dirge-like filler track! Personally, I am quite fond of the piece, which is appealingly different to anything else on the record.

'No Fun' (The Stooges)
Scott's drums introduce this next number briefly before the rest of the band join in with Ron's monster riff soon taking charge. Some delightfully characterful handclaps also accompany the instrumentation, adding a real sheen to proceedings. Iggy then takes centre stage, coming across like a punkier version of Mick Jagger.

Reportedly, Ron originally came up with two chords and repeatedly played them over and over. Iggy liked the riff and thought the band should do something with it. According to Iggy, in interviews, he also used Johnny Cash's 'I Walk The Line' as a model/structure to develop the song. The middle eight is also Stones influenced (indeed, Iggy has freely admitted that he used a lot from The Stones (and The Velvet Underground) in general). Ron's distinctively distorted lead guitar sounds accompany Iggy's primal wails of 'Well c'mon!' towards the end of the song, which makes for a very effective combination and a fitting conclusion to the song.

Lyrically, it is the perfect archetypal youth anthem of boredom and alienation, with Iggy having stated that he wanted to make a song about how they were living in the Midwest and what their life was about.

History has also clearly proved that this was a seminal proto-punk tune with the song having gone on to inspire many later punk bands. The Sex Pistols went on to record this number as the B-side to their 'Pretty Vacant' single, whilst The Damned also performed this track live in their late-1970s heyday.

The 'full' version of the song was later included as a bonus track on the 2005/10 reissues.

'Real Cool Time' (The Stooges)

Ron's lively wah-wah guitar sounds initiate this next number with solid rhythmic support from Scott and Dave, creating a heavy, psychedelic ambience before Iggy's vocals commence. As per the band's usual modus operandi on this album, Ron's relentless lead guitar sounds drive the song along at a bruising pace before the tune culminates with an even noisier and more frenetic demonstration of Ron's guitar work.

This is one of the three tracks supposedly written in 24 hours by the band when in desperate need of more material for the album. Ron again came up with the riff for the song whilst Iggy provided the rather minimal lyrical content. He apparently saw it as a 'booty call' song, but just from one side of the phone conversation. In the liner notes to the 2007 *Escaped Maniacs* DVD, Iggy said of recording 'Real Cool Time' that the ambition had been to make 'music that sounded like a bunch of little Tartar tribesmen sweeping along the desert on their ponies, ready to bring savage visitation to all in their path, yet the vocal is almost floating over that.'

The tune is pretty slight overall, coming in at around two-and-a-half minutes in length, and betrays its 'written overnight' origins. However, it still proffers a reasonably fun listen.

'Ann' (The Stooges)

A slower tempo, dark ballad-style number is up next, offering a nice change of pace. This one also exudes a Doors-ish vibe. Scott's drum work is dominant on this one, whilst Ron's distorted guitar sounds are used more sparingly here and are slightly more set back in the background, at least initially. This effectively generates a more haunted and unsettled ambience. Near the end of the song, Ron and Scott begin a duel for dominance behind Iggy. Meanwhile, Iggy's crooning vocals are a delight, even if his croon actually gets a little more frightening and threatening at one point! The song eventually comes to a climax with a big instrumental cacophony.

Some sources state that this more melancholic-sounding number apparently evolved out of an earlier musical jam piece by the band called 'The Dance Of Romance'. The focus of the song is also a little uncertain, with various sources offering different suggestions. Some see it as an ode to the Ashetons' mother, Ann, whilst others think it perhaps refers to another Ann Arbor acquaintance of the band. It could also be an ode to the band's hometown of Ann Arbor.

The 'full' version of the song was included as a bonus track on the 2005/10 reissues (which includes nearly six minutes of 'The Dance Of Romance').

'Not Right' (The Stooges)
The drums, guitars and vocals pretty much start together, with the ensuing combination of Ron's dirty and grimy-sounding guitar work and Iggy's vocals resulting in an infectious and compelling number. Indeed, Ron seems to be having a lot of fun with his effects pedals here, as the distorted lead guitar sounds dominate the instrumentation once again, whilst Iggy's vocal delivery is suitably matter-of-fact throughout. Lyrically, this one is about people initially thinking that they want to be with someone (based on their looks or immediate attraction) who is, ultimately, 'not right' for them for whatever reason.

Another track written at the 'last minute' for the album, Ron reportedly wrote most of the music whilst Iggy again worked out the lyrics. Indeed, Scott Asheton later alleged that 'Not Right' was actually performed for the first time at the actual recording session.

Again, this tune betrays its 'written last minute' status somewhat, but it still serves up a reasonably enjoyable listening experience.

'Little Doll' (The Stooges)
Some tasty bass sounds kickstart this one briefly before full-band instrumentation starts up. Iggy proceeds to sneer and snarl away, whilst Scott pummels away, Ron riffs away, and Dave slaps away on this decent little rocker. It is fun, but the tune here is a little derivative of earlier tracks on the album (indeed, the riff is reminiscent of the one found in '1969', albeit slowed down a bit). Ron's wah-wah lead guitar sounds, backed by Scott's solid drum pounding and Dave's heavy, chugging bass work, eventually see the song out in style.

Interestingly, the bass line here was reportedly 'borrowed' from the song 'Upper Egypt And Lower Egypt' by Pharoah Sanders, the jazz saxophonist, and offers a nice rhythmic groove to the piece. The band would, of course, go on to pursue their avant-garde/free jazz interests more earnestly on their next album, but it's interesting to see this early influence in play. [Some sources also allege that 'Little Doll' was developed out of an earlier live number by The Stooges entitled 'Goodbye Bozos'.]

To be honest, this and the other two songs written at the 'last minute' to expand the album are probably (and perhaps unsurprisingly) the weakest tracks on the record, but they are all still fun and perfectly listenable.

Other Contemporary Song
'Asthma Attack' (The Stooges)
This rather frightening and intense-sounding piece is full of free-form instrumental noise and primal vocal sounds. Iggy serves up a concoction of screams and other weird and random vocal sounds, whilst Ron lays on the feedback-laden guitar sounds, Scott throws in frantic and seemingly random drum rolls and Dave dishes up some discordant bass lines. It certainly makes for a disconcerting cacophony and was quite rightly, in my humble opinion, left off the final album! However, it is definitely interesting to listen to since it's probably similar in feel/style to the band's earliest stabs at music when they were all about improv and homemade instruments (circa late 1967/early 1968). It is also probably the closest we will ever get to hearing the pre-professional studio Stooges! However, at over six minutes in length, this is quite hard work to get through!

A 'song' with this title was actually a staple of the group's early live shows when they focussed on arty experimentation in noisy and chaotic feedback/improv. However, this studio version (allegedly) may not actually be the same composition that was played live.

This track appeared as a bonus track on the 2010 Collectors' Edition of the album.

Fun House (1970)

Personnel:
Iggy Pop: vocals
Dave Alexander: bass
Ron Asheton: guitar
Scott Asheton: drums
Steve Mackay: tenor saxophone
Recorded at Elektra Sound Recorders, Los Angeles, California (May 1970)
Produced by Don Gallucci
UK release date: December 1970
US release date: July 1970
Chart places: UK: did not chart, US: did not chart

After the band's debut album release, they continued to tour extensively (the band performed mostly in the Michigan area, but plenty of gigs were now being undertaken further afield across the US), honing their stagecraft and musicality somewhat. As 1969 turned into 1970, the band began writing material for the next album. As mentioned previously, the band felt that the true power and potency of their sound had been diluted somewhat on their debut album (with Elektra's insistence that they compose more structured songs), so this time around, they set out to make the record they wanted.

The band also approached this next album with some new additional influences and frames of reference. Whilst Ron continued to be influenced by the likes of Jimi Hendrix and The Who (which ultimately inspired him to come up with some memorable riffs for the next LP), Iggy had been listening to jazz and funk records and this filtered through to the new music. Specific influences included the free jazz of John Coltrane and Archie Shepp, whilst the funk of James Brown also helped shape the new record (the jazz influences had, in part, come courtesy of John Sinclair (MC5 manager), who was a big fan of free jazz).

In the liner notes to *1970: The Complete Fun House Sessions*, Ron Asheton said:

> We all loved John Coltrane. When we heard The Doors' record [*The Soft Parade*, with sax solos by Curtis Amy], we thought we could do it better – so we got Steve Mackay, who was a cool guy and a great saxophone player.

From the same liner notes, Iggy Pop said:

> I was listening to James Brown and a lot of Coltrane. What James Brown was coming up with at that time, with 'Say it Loud, I'm Black and I'm Proud', 'Make it Funky' and 'I Can't Stand Myself', was just minimal, high-steppin', badass rock music, and that upped the ante … I wanted something badder based on that.

Regarding the recruitment of tenor saxophonist Steve Mackay, it was circa February/March 1970 that Iggy became aware of the Michigan-based musician and subsequently decided that he wanted him to play on the new record. Therefore, in April, just two days before the band were due to leave for Los Angeles to begin recording the new album, Iggy called Steve up and requested his presence at the forthcoming sessions (coincidentally, at this time, Steve was also working at the Discount Records store that Iggy had once worked at) with the view that sax would add more depth to the band's music and a new free/avant-garde jazz dimension to the musical proceedings. Also, around springtime, Mackay made his first live appearances with the band.

Elektra staff producer Don Gallucci was selected as producer for the new album. As with Cale before, the band were very happy with this choice as not only had Don played keyboards on The Kingsmen's classic 'Louie Louie' (which the band loved), but Don had also been part of Don and The Goodtimes, who had effectively been the house band on Dick Clark's TV show *Where The Action Is* in the mid-1960s – this had also impressed the Stooges.

Recording sessions commenced at Elektra Sound Recorders studio in May and reportedly started with a conventional studio setup; that is, the amps and drums were placed in a heavily baffled room, Iggy used a studio microphone on a boom and everyone wore headphones, etc. However, using this approach reportedly led to disappointing early sonic results. Therefore, the band tried a new tactic whereby the sonic baffling was removed from the walls and the band were allowed to set up in the same room as they would do for a stage performance, thus enabling them to feed off each other's performance. For the album, Gallucci wanted to ensure that the band's live energy came across, so the band were essentially recorded live in the studio with minimal or no overdubs. Iggy performed his vocals through a hand-held microphone with PA speakers providing the vocal foldback. This setup subsequently proved conducive to a more positive band atmosphere. Numerous takes of each song were then recorded, with lyrics and tempos varying until the band were happy.

Don also designed the recording sessions so that a particular song was worked on/recorded per day, in order of the band's actual live set (as mentioned, the *Fun House* songs had been developed and played live as and when they had been written and completed before the commencement of the recording sessions). The final track listing is almost their live show in the correct running order – however, although 'Loose' started the live set and was intended as the album opener, the powers that be thought that 'Down On The Street' would ultimately make for a better opening track.

Drug-wise, the *Fun House* album, like the debut, had essentially been written on marijuana and psychedelics, but by the end of the recording, cocaine had entered the band scene, to be followed a short while later by heroin (although not all band members succumbed to the temptation of heroin, as Ron, reportedly, managed to resist). However, the addition of cocaine and heroin to the existing regime of weed, speed and LSD proved disastrous and this is when the band's drug use started to become a real problem.

When the record was released, the band and record company alike had high hopes for the album. However, with mixed critical reviews, poor sales and limited radio play, the LP flopped badly. Lester Bangs (writing for either *Creem* or *The Village Voice* – sources vary) had this to say about the *Fun House* album:

> It is as loose and raw an album as we've ever had ... *Fun House* is one of those rare albums that never sits still long enough to actually solidify into what it previously seemed. Not always immediately accessible, it might take some getting into, but the time spent is well repaid.

However, Lester Bangs was not the only big supporter of the band at the time. There were others in the music press, but unfortunately, radio play was poor and the public generally remained unimpressed. Other mixed press reviews included the following: *New Musical Express* (*NME*) (not exactly fans of the band!), December 1970: 'If you can make virtue out of reasonably played rock tunes, sung by a tortured non-voice over repetitive riffs, then *Fun House* is for you.' *Melody Maker*, December 1970: 'It's a muddy load of sluggish, unimaginative rubbish ... There's really no excuse for turning out such bloody rotten stuff.' *Rolling Stone*: 'The new record is much more sophisticated than their first. And you cannot deny that they are the best Detroit area rock band.'

However, over the past 50 years, *Fun House* has subsequently and belatedly become (quite rightfully) acknowledged as an incredibly influential album, especially on the subsequent punk, new wave, grunge and alternative music scenes. The album now boasts many music celebrity fans, including the likes of Jack White, who described *Fun House* (in the 2005 *Fun House* CD reissue liner notes) as 'the very definition of Detroit rock 'n' roll, and by proxy, the definitive rock album of America.' Henry Rollins, in *Rolling Stone* in 2020, had this to say about the record as it turned 50 in 2020: 'Rarely can you say that a record is perfect. But *Fun House* is perfect.'

With the *Fun House* album, the band certainly succeeded in their ambition of demonstrating a little more musical sophistication than had been displayed on their debut album. James Brown-influenced funky guitar and sax riffs help elevate the musicality. Indeed, the album fuses free jazz, garage rock, r&b and blues and delivers it in the band's familiar brutal and ferocious manner. Ron's guitar work has improved somewhat since the debut, with more technical prowess on display and, as a result, he delivers a far more confident performance. Scott and Dave, meanwhile, continue to provide a viciously pounding backdrop, and Iggy's vocal delivery is more honed than before as evidenced by his more mature and considered performances (all of the touring between the first two albums had certainly helped improve the band's technical proficiencies, as well as their general confidence levels).

Ultimately, the record proffers an even heavier-sounding listen than their debut, impassioned and full of the band's attitude. It is also worth highlighting Steve Mackay's contribution, too. His presence on the latter part of the record certainly lends it an avant-garde, jazz vibe. For me, the first five songs are absolutely great, but with the introduction of Mackay's sax, we suddenly veer into increasingly free-form jazz-rock territory, which, in all honesty, is not exactly to my taste. By the end of 'L.A. Blues', it's rather a welcome relief that proceedings have come to an end, which is a shame because the first five songs are terrific (and a noted improvement over the debut songwriting efforts). Of course, I am sure there are many, many fans out there who would disagree with me and argue that the jazzier aspects make the album so appealing. Ah, well, different strokes for different folks!

As with their debut record, this sophomore effort has made *Rolling Stone*'s '500 Greatest Albums of All Time' lists and, indeed, regularly features in many critics' polls.

Post-recording, the band continued to tour and, in June 1970, performed their *Fun House* set at the Cincinnati Summer Pop Festival. This event was filmed for TV and a couple of Stooges numbers were subsequently broadcast nationally later in August. This now-legendary footage features Iggy surfing over the audience, carried along outstretched palms (Iggy had apparently tried out this crowd surfing once before back in March, also in Cincinnati), whilst smearing peanut butter over himself and throwing chunks of it into the crowd (apparently, someone in the crowd simply handed him a jar of peanut butter). As usual, Iggy appeared shirtless, wearing torn jeans, silver lamé gloves and a dog collar around his neck. Post-TV exposure, the band unsurprisingly picked up some media attention for this performance!

On 8 August 1970, the band also performed at the Goose Lake International Music Festival. This infamous gig found Iggy in a particularly bad way due to (allegedly) ingesting some bad cocaine a few hours beforehand, resulting in temporary amnesia just before showtime. Apparently, Iggy regained his mind just in time for the performance. However, Dave Alexander was also in a particularly bad way, either stoned or drunk, or both, which resulted in Dave being unable to play his bass guitar throughout the show. This proved to be the straw that broke the camel's back with regard to Dave's position in the band. Things had already been brewing for a while with Dave due to his increasingly erratic and unreliable behaviour and commitment to the band, but after his dismal performance at the festival, Iggy promptly sacked the bassist.

Band roadie Zeke Zettner was then recruited as Dave's replacement, whilst shortly after, another band roadie (and long-time band friend), Bill Cheatham, joined as second guitarist (Bill had also been to high school with Iggy and Ron, and had also played with The Dirty Shames with Ron, Scott and Dave before The Stooges). More gigs followed with this new lineup (from August – October/November, until the last gigs with Steve Mackay/Bill Cheatham). Mid-August, in particular, saw a mini-residency at Ungano's nightclub in New

York, which effectively served as a showcase launch for the new *Fun House* LP. Live, the band were now firing on all cylinders and reaching a zenith, whilst Iggy continued to up the frontman ante with wild antics – such as pouring hot melted candle wax onto his chest – that continued to shock and transfix audiences across the nation.

[Note: Regarding Steve Mackay's departure, the band, circa October 1970, were now looking to move away from the free jazz stylings of the *Fun House* record and so dispensed with his services. Mackay initially returned to work at Discount Records before becoming involved in a variety of jazz projects. He would eventually rejoin The Stooges in 2003 for their Coachella reunion gig.]

Late November saw the entrance of James Williamson onto the band scene, as he replaced Bill Cheatham as second guitarist. James was born in Castroville, Texas (29 October 1949) and had first become aware of Iggy, Ron and Co. circa 1966. Post *Fun House*, he even ended up living with some of the Stooge family. This subsequently led to the Texan guitarist being formally welcomed into the band. In December, there were further band personnel changes afoot, as Zeke Zettner also left the band (to be later replaced by Jimmy Recca).

Again, as with the debut album, there have been many reissues over the years. 1999 also saw the release of *1970: The Complete Fun House Sessions* – a seven-disc behemoth of a set chronicling, in every detail, the making of the album (released via Rhino Handmade/Elektra). Initially distributed with a limited print run, it was reissued digitally in 2005 and then eventually reissued on CD in all its glory in 2010. Only for the truly hardiest fan, this set runs for nearly eight hours! Every take from every session, in order, is featured, including not only all the music but also all the studio dialogue, jokes, false starts, etc. It should be noted that, if nothing else, this mammoth set reveals the band to be a lot more focused, methodical and disciplined in the studio than perhaps their reputation would have us believe – they come across as a very professional and hard-working unit. The set also reveals how Iggy's lyrics tended to evolve through multiple takes, thus shining a light on his skill as a lyrical improviser.

Also, like the band's first album, Elektra/Rhino issued a two-CD set in 2005 containing a second disc of bonus tracks (14 tracks culled from the *Complete Sessions* box). In 2020, Elektra issued a 50th-anniversary deluxe vinyl box set which included 15 LPs, including the original album remastered at 45 RPM, *1970: The Complete Fun House Sessions* and *Have Some Fun: Live At Ungano's* (17 August 1970 gig). In addition, the set showcased two 7" singles ('Down On The Street' b/w 'I Feel Alright (1970)' – one in a French picture sleeve, the other in an Elektra company sleeve) and a plethora of ephemera.

'Down On The Street' (The Stooges)
A lively and pulsating guitar and drum fusion introduces the album to listeners, closely followed by Iggy's vocal wails before the song's lyrical

content begins properly with the great line, 'Down on the street where the faces shine'. Ron's driving, heavy, blues-inspired riff work, backed by Scott and Dave's pounding rhythmic sounds, propels the song forward, whereupon, at around the two-minute mark, Ron lets rip with a terrific wah-wah solo which squeals and squawks away. Iggy continues to yelp and whoop in the background whilst listeners are treated to his encouraging shouts of 'Come on' during the compelling chorus. Indeed, throughout the song, Iggy sounds both menacing and animalistic as he snarls and growls his way through the piece. The song eventually comes to a somewhat abrupt end rather than a subtle fade-out. However, this is a great, brutal-sounding opening to the album.

Originally entitled 'Down On The Beach' and conceived as a love song for Iggy's wife at the time, it was later reworked into 'Down On The Street' (also, because the band hadn't actually been to the beach, they decided that they were more down on the street!). Lyrically, Iggy was apparently inspired by his acid trips at the time, whereby he would take everything in whilst walking around the streets.

The single mix of the track differs slightly from the album version in that it boasts a distinctive organ overdub that pervades the track (allegedly performed by producer Don Gallucci and without the band's knowledge). There is absolutely nothing wrong with this (indeed, one could argue that it adds a little more flavour to the song), but, in all honesty, it is not entirely necessary. I guess Elektra probably approved of this as it inevitably gives the track more of a Doors vibe (who were, of course, the Stooges' label mates at the time). This single mix is also much shorter at just over two-and-a-half minutes. The LP version runs for a little under four minutes.

The single was released in the US in July 1970 backed with fellow album track 'I Feel Alright (1970)'. The single was also released in France and Japan with the same B-side. This single mix was made available on both the *Complete Sessions* box and the 2005 double CD reissue.

Numerous takes of this tune are available on the *Complete Sessions* box, where one can appreciate all the tempo experimentation that occurred. Takes 1 and 8 were also presented as bonus tracks on the 2005 double disc reissue of the album.

'Down On The Street' has been covered by various artists, including Rage Against the Machine.

'Loose' (The Stooges)

Another exuberant guitar/drum intro combined with further Iggy yelping opens this next number, another driving rocker. Iggy's call of 'Now look out!' indicates that it's time for the song to erupt and the rest of the band respond accordingly. Ron's blazing riff work shines again whilst Iggy impresses with his sneering vocal, informing listeners that 'I'll stick it deep inside, 'cause I'm loose!' Yep, the lyrics leave nothing to the imagination! Meanwhile, Scott and Dave have to work incredibly hard to keep pace whilst backing Ron's relentless wah-wah guitar work, which makes for a great instrumental sound throughout the entire piece. This is all enhanced by the equally compelling vocal performance from Iggy, too, which oozes sleazily from the speakers.

This appealingly sordid track (reportedly about the music business being like the underworld) maintains a highly energetic tempo throughout and was chiefly written by Ron (music) and Iggy (lyrics).

Numerous takes of the song are available on the *Complete Sessions* box, where one can appreciate the lyrics developing over the various takes. The demo and takes 2 and 22 are also included as bonus tracks on the 2005 CD reissue of the album.

'T.V. Eye' (The Stooges)

An almighty roar of 'Lord!' from Iggy signals the start of this next tune, whereupon Ron starts up his monstrous riff backed by his brother's drum skin battering. Further wails ensue before Iggy proceeds to lasciviously deliver the song's lyrical content. The relentlessly paced, no-frills proto-punk instrumentation continues with the rhythm section barely maintaining control in the background. Around the two-minute mark, Ron lets rip with some terrific licks whilst Iggy unleashes his inner beast as he screams and growls away in untamed fashion. It's a fantastic duel between the pair of them and they both more than hold their own. Momentarily, the song then comes to a complete stop before Ron quickly starts up his riff motor again. Iggy soon rejoins the picture and Scott's kit is brought more to the fore during this latter part of the song. Finally, a brief flourish of wah-wah-infused distortion brings the song to a satisfying close. All in all, this song stands as an excellent showcase for the band and its brutal-sounding and electrifying brand of rock 'n' roll.

The song was developed out of an initial bluesy riff idea that Ron had come up with. Iggy liked the riff and wanted the band to develop a song out of it. The song's title (which came from Iggy) was reportedly partly inspired by the CBS logo, which Iggy felt was like a big eye staring out at him from his TV. However, the lyric, 'She got a TV eye on me', apparently references a term that the Ashetons' sister used to refer to guys she fancied (apparently, it referred to a look someone gave to somebody that they were attracted to). The song was also known as 'See That Cat' at some point, according to the *Complete Sessions* box.

Numerous takes of the song are available on the *Complete Sessions* box. Takes 7 and 8 were also included as a bonus track on the 2005 album reissue.

'Dirt' (The Stooges)

A Scott drum roll initiates this next number, a beautifully sleazy, sexy, slow-burning blues-rock groove of a song! Boasting another great world-weary Iggy vocal throughout, this darkly seductive tune also finds Iggy supported by some suitably atmospheric instrumentation. Ron's superlative wah-wah-infused guitar work (particularly his mid-song solo) is aided admirably by Scott and Dave throughout. A splendidly dirty-sounding blues rock tune, this epic enjoys a seven-minute runtime and not once does it threaten to bore or outstay its welcome.

Dave Alexander came up with the riff for this one and his wonderful and iconic bassline underpins the entire song. Iggy's vocal delivery, meanwhile, is slightly more measured, which perfectly suits the slower, more laid-back tempo. The song, lyrically, essentially reflects the band's attitude to life at the time:

> Ooh, I been dirt
> And I don't care
> Ooh, I've been hurt
> But I don't care

An obvious precursor to grunge, this track has been covered by a variety of other artists, a particular favourite of mine being the version by Depeche Mode.

Numerous takes of the song are available on the *Complete Sessions* box. Take four is also available on the 2005 CD album reissue as a bonus track.

'1970' (The Stooges)

Another frenzied instrumental onslaught ignites this next number. Ron is almost at full throttle from the off as he starts up his crunchy riff. Iggy throws in some primal whooping whilst Scott initiates his urgent, up-tempo drum beat. With Dave adding a muscular bass line, the quartet seemingly battle each other for dominance. The noise they make here is ferocious and awe-inspiring. The song then hurtles along at breakneck speed until around the two-minute mark, when Ron lets rip with a howling wah-wah-treated solo. Then, around the three-and-a-half-minute mark, listeners are surprised by the sudden entrance of a jazzy saxophone, courtesy of Steve Mackay, whose sax sounds certainly add a new, unexpected dimension to the musical proceedings. Upon entering the fray, Mackay then does his very best to win the battle for instrumental dominance. Against this cacophonous instrumentation, Iggy continues to rage away, screaming, 'I feel alright!' before the band, exhausted, finally come to a halt at just over the five-minute mark.

Also known as 'I Feel Alright', Ron again came up with the riff for this one. It is another terrifically swaggering rocker that provided clear inspiration for future punk, grunge and noise rockers. Original Damned guitarist Brian James once described the song's riff as 'instant mayhem' to *Ultimate Classic Rock*. Indeed, The Damned even covered the track on their debut album.

The single mix runs to a little over three minutes in length compared to the full album version, which runs a couple of minutes longer.

Numerous takes of the song are available on the *Complete Sessions* box. The single mix was made available on both the *Complete Sessions* box and the

2005 double CD album reissue. Take three is also available on the 2005 reissue as a bonus track.

'Fun House' (The Stooges)
Bass sounds and handclaps briefly initiate the album's title track before the rest of the band join in, with Iggy's vocal whoops and Mackay's sax quickly dominating the relatively free-form jam cacophony. Listeners are treated to over a minute of this discordance before Iggy instructs the rest of the band to 'bring it down'. The song then begins to settle down a bit (just a bit, mind!) as Iggy's vocals commence battle against the sax-dominated instrumental background. Ron's wah-wah guitar work attempts to come to the fore at the post-four-minute mark, but Mackay's sax still ultimately dominates the musical proceedings (whilst Scott also desperately attempts to hold everything together with his drumming). All hell then breaks loose during the last two minutes of the track as everyone goes crazy. Iggy's vocals sound positively unhinged, Mackay's free jazz sax sounds run amok, Ron throws in some scorching licks and Scott frantically thrashes his drum skins. This dissonance, thankfully, eventually begins to wind down and ultimately comes to a (slightly welcome!) end at around the post-seven-minute and 30-second mark. Overall, this is a very noisy, jam-style number with an obvious avant-garde jazz influence.

Reportedly the last song to be written for the album, it was Dave Alexander who came up with the riff/bass melody that underpins the entire piece. It was also named after the band's infamous communal headquarters in Ann Arbor.

Numerous takes of the song are available on the *Complete Sessions* box. Takes 2 and 3 are also available on the 2005 CD album reissue as bonus tracks.

'L.A. Blues' (The Stooges)
An angry-sounding noise of vocal screams, screeching sax, wailing guitar and bombastic drum beats introduces this closing number and then proceeds to continue endlessly! Discordant instrumentation backs up Iggy's animalistic and guttural vocal sounds throughout this deranged, melody-free freak-out. This din drags on for approximately five minutes before the band wind things down and the album finally comes to a close.

The band were reportedly encouraged to reproduce their end-of-live set (improvised) mayhem for this closing number; Steve Mackay reckons they all dropped acid in order to achieve the proper mood for this! The John Coltrane influence is also obvious on this free-form/free jazz jam freak-out.

Numerous takes of the track are available on the *Complete Sessions* box, where the track was originally known as 'Freak'. However, it takes a brave person to listen to the full 17+ minute first take, available on the *Complete Fun House Sessions* box!

Other Contemporary Songs
'Lost In The Future' (The Stooges)
A slow tempo and a hypnotic guitar and drum fusion launch this number before a more restrained, albeit still quite raw-sounding, Iggy vocal is showcased. The mesmeric tempo is then maintained throughout, resulting in a rather beguiling tune. The sound of a sax is featured just before the two-minute mark, which adds character to the piece in this instance, rather than being overbearing, and Mackay subtly weaves his sax licks in and around the other minimalist instrumental sounds. This relatively sedate tune then continues until the band wrap things up at just under the six-minute mark. Overall, this is a rather interesting and atmospheric number, which features an effectively impassioned Iggy vocal performance, too. Personally, I would have preferred to see this track on the final released album rather than something like 'L.A. Blues'. Only a few takes of this number were ever undertaken in the studio, but I think it showed a lot of promise and potential.

The various takes of this tune are available on the *1970: The Complete Fun House Sessions* box. Take one is also available on the 2005 CD album reissue. According to the liner notes in the *Complete Sessions* box, the unfinished 'Lost In The Future' track was a surprise find to all parties involved.

'Slide (Slidin' The Blues)' (The Stooges)
This is nothing more than a fun run-through of a basic blues-style rock jam. Ron battles with Mackay again for musical dominance (howling blues guitar licks versus jazzy sax notes) whilst Iggy mainly recites the song's title. Scott, meanwhile, contributes a slow, sympathetic drum beat. Overall, this is fine and mildly interesting but ultimately inconsequential.

Again, this tune is available on the *Complete Fun House Sessions* box. Take one is also available on the 2005 CD album reissue.

Raw Power (1973)

Personnel:
Iggy Pop: vocals
James Williamson: guitars
Ron Asheton: bass, vocals
Scott Asheton: drums
Recorded at CBS Studios, London (September/October 1972)
Produced by Iggy Pop, mixed by David Bowie and Iggy Pop
UK release date: June 1973
US release date: February 1973 (although there is debate about the month of US release. Other sources state March and May as possible release months)
Chart places: UK: did not chart (note: the 1977 reissue did chart at number 44), US: 182

After the commercial failure of *Fun House*, the band slowly but surely began its initial decline. Iggy and certain other band members sank further into the clutches of their respective drug (heroin) habits, and during the second half of 1970, there were several personnel changes. By the spring of 1971, the lineup now consisted of Iggy, Ron, Scott, James Williamson and Jimmy Recca. This lineup performed a spring tour, with gigs full of new songs (written by Iggy). However, this particular lineup never made it into a studio to record any of the material at the time. At some point, Elektra visited the band to check out some of this new material with a view to a third album. However, they had not been overly impressed by what they heard or, indeed, by what they saw, with most of the band well and truly crippled by drugs. One of the visiting Elektra folk was also very upset at seeing Ron's Nazi memorabilia collection! (Ron was a Nazi memorabilia collector and often wore Nazi uniforms, etc. There was nothing political about this; Ron was just genuinely interested in Nazi stuff and thought the outfits looked cool!) However, whatever the reasons, all this was in addition to the already present disappointment over sales of the *Fun House* LP (it had sold less than the debut). It was, therefore, not that much of a surprise when Elektra ended up dropping the band instead of pursuing a third album.

Towards the very end of May, things had gotten so bad that Iggy and James quit the band, leaving the remaining trio to perform one last contracted gig in July (where they performed a mainly instrumental set, although, for one song, they did pull a guy from the audience to sing vocals). The band thus disbanded for the time being.

At some point, post-band disintegration, Iggy headed off to New York with hopes that he could yet salvage his career. As fortune would have it, there happened to be a big Iggy fan in New York circa September 1971 who very much wanted to meet him – a certain gentleman by the name of David Bowie! Bowie was in New York with his manager, Tony DeFries, to sign his own RCA record deal, but whilst there, a meeting was also set up with Iggy.

Everyone got on and discussions soon ensued about them working together. Ultimately, Iggy ended up signing with GEM as a solo artist (in early 1972, the MainMan group would be set up by DeFries as a spin-off company from GEM, which subsequently took control of artists such as Bowie and Iggy, etc.) with Bowie/DeFries promising him that they would find a suitable British backing band to work with him.

Once signed, Iggy was told to sit and wait for the call to come over to England. However, during this period, Iggy reconnected with old Stooges pal James Williamson, whereupon he suggested that James should come over to England with him to work on his new album. In the meantime, DeFries also managed to get Iggy a deal with Columbia Records (again, as a solo artist). Ultimately, the other band members never signed with MainMan or Columbia. However, because of the returning Stooges, the *Raw Power* record was eventually released and credited to Iggy and The Stooges). Thus, it was in the spring of 1972 that Iggy and James both flew over to England to begin work on a solo Iggy record. Once in England, as promised by Bowie and DeFries, a British backing band/rhythm section was sought, but no one suitable was found. Reportedly, they were not aggressive enough for Iggy and James, so the pair decided to call up the Asheton brothers and get them over.

The Ashetons arrived in June and preliminary rehearsals took place with the band tackling some of the new songs that had been composed by Iggy and James. Although Ron had seemingly been 'demoted' to bass and, indeed, with both brothers feeling some resentment at being treated like sidemen in their own band, Ron and Scott still created a formidable rhythmic foundation. Initial rehearsals were undertaken at RG Jones Studios (Wimbledon) before the band then decamped to Trident Studios to work on demos of songs like 'I Got A Right', 'Gimme Some Skin', 'I'm Sick Of You', 'Scene Of The Crime' and 'Tight Pants', etc.

Finally, in mid-July 1972, the reconstituted band performed live again in front of an audience. This showcase gig took place at King's Cross Cinema (London) and was the gig where legendary rock music photographer Mick Rock took his now-iconic photos of the band, and in particular, Iggy, replete with platinum blonde hair, tight silver leather trousers and copious amounts of face make-up, with one of the images ultimately ending up as the front cover of the *Raw Power* LP. However, regarding the iconic cover, Iggy was reportedly not initially keen on it and had no creative input. It was only later in life that he grew to appreciate how cool the cover was. (Incidentally, future punk legends John Lydon and Mick Jones were apparently both in attendance at this gig, too.)

A couple of days later, the band undertook some slightly more formal recording sessions at Olympic Studios (London) with Keith Harwood (Rolling Stones engineer) helping out. Again, some of the new song demos were worked on. However, Tony DeFries was reportedly not at all keen on what the band had been working on and rejected the material, feeling the band could and should do better (indeed, DeFries reportedly suggested that the album follow a more conventional structure; that is, a fast, up-tempo opener for each side followed by a ballad, a classic rocker and then a moodier closing number). At the time, David Bowie also offered to produce the record, but Iggy refused the offer and insisted on producing it alone.

Although ultimately not released at the time, some of these pre-*Raw Power* songs did eventually see the light of day in 1977 when a couple of singles were released: 'I Got A Right' b/w 'Gimme Some Skin' was released via Siamese Records, and 'I'm Sick Of You' b/w 'Tight Pants' and 'Scene Of The Crime' was released via BOMP! Both releases were warmly welcomed by the burgeoning punk community at the time. Additional note: the July 'Olympic' sessions have also subsequently been released, most notably by Easy Action, on their *Heavy Liquid* box set in 2005 – please refer to the later Further Related And Recommended Albums And Songs section for more detailed information.

Following DeFries' rejection of the initial material, the band (well, Iggy and James, that is) subsequently returned to the drawing board and came up with some new offerings. Essentially, the way the pair worked would be that James would come up with an initial riff, and then Iggy would come up with the first part of a vocal line and the songs would develop and grow from there. James Williamson spoke to *Classic Rock* in 2018 about the process:

Generally, the way we worked between Jim and I was that I would come up with a riff, we'd get together and he'd come up with the lyrics, and then we'd go back and forth and mould a song out of that. Generally speaking, I wrote those riffs in my room on an acoustic guitar.

Around this time, MainMan became rather busy and preoccupied with trying to break its golden boy, Bowie, in the US. This meant that Iggy and Co. were essentially left to their own devices. So, the band ended up taking their newly written material into the studio and simply got on with the job of recording the new album (September/October 1972, CBS Studios). According to some sources, drink and drugs allegedly helped fuel the wild sessions, although other sources (James Williamson included) reckon the band were pretty straight during their UK sojourn. Either way, productivity was good. Indeed, the earlier rehearsal/studio sessions helped ensure that the band were well and truly 'in the zone.' Reportedly, there were only six to 12 takes required for the *Raw Power* songs, certainly nothing too excessive like there had been on the previous *Fun House* LP. Again, this was probably because the songs had been more rehearsed beforehand and a little more finalised before the recording took place.

By early October, the album was done and dusted, but due to MainMan being kept busy with Ziggy, nothing actually happened for a while. Therefore, the band ended up heading back to the US, eventually staying in a house in the Hollywood Hills at MainMan's expense.

Regarding the mixing of the album, Iggy had apparently already turned in a couple of rough mixes of the album, but either Tony DeFries or Columbia/ CBS (or both) had been left unimpressed. Therefore, David Bowie was invited to remix the record in Hollywood in late 1972 (with Messrs Pop and Williamson also attending some of the mixing sessions). On the final released product, the mixing credit went to both Bowie and Iggy.

Some of Iggy's initial rough mixes eventually appeared on the *Rough Power* album release (Bomp!, 1994). Whilst not particularly better or worse than the 1973 released mixes, they are noticeably different. Of *Rough Power* and the subsequent Bowie/Pop released mixes, Iggy had this to say in the *Raw Power* reissue liner notes:

Somebody's since put out something on Bomp, *Rough Power*, which were some of my original mixes, but I think what David and I came up with at these [original remix] sessions was better than that. So I think he helped the thing. I'm very proud of the eccentric, odd little record that came out.

Another Iggy quote from the 1997 reissue liner notes reasserted his retrospective feelings:

In retrospect, I think the little touches Bowie put on the mix helped and I think some of the things MainMan did helped, and more than anything else, what the whole experience did was to get me out of Detroit and onto a world stage.

Once the mixing had been completed, the band again became bored and restless waiting for the release of the album (and, indeed, any news from MainMan), with various members sinking further into their debauched lifestyles. The band did, however, still manage to write and rehearse new material during this extended period of debauchery.

Finally, a showcase (homecoming) gig was booked for the end of March 1973 at Detroit's Ford Auditorium. Circa February (and in order to add a more rootsy sound to the band's music), Iggy recruited ex-Prime Mover keyboardist Bob Sheff for the forthcoming showcase gig. The ensuing gig was apparently a triumph. However, post-gig, James Williamson found himself being sacked (temporarily, as it turned out) for bad behaviour (although this was probably due to management pressure). Indeed, not long after this gig, circa spring 1973, a rapidly deteriorating relationship (not helped by the drug-fuelled bad behaviour of the band at this time) saw MainMan decide to drop Iggy (and the band) completely. However, this obviously had major repercussions for the new album. As a result of MainMan withdrawing their support, the record label, Columbia, ultimately did not put too much effort into the promotion of the new record, the unsurprising result being a flop record.

Sources differ as to when the LP was finally released in the US (February/ March/May 1973 are all contender months), but regardless, the album bombed. Ironically, this time around, the music press critics had been generous with its praise. *Creem* said that 'Only a truly diabolical mind could have made the best album of the 70s and Iggy apparently has it because he's summed everything up in nine songs.' *Rolling Stone* were equally positive: 'With *Raw Power*, The Stooges return with a vengeance, exhibiting all the ferocity that characterised them at their livid best.'

Regarding the *Raw Power* LP, Iggy admitted in subsequent interviews that he knew it would finish his career commercially, even before they recorded it, but at that point, he just did not give a damn! He was right – the album bombed.

Iggy's thoughts on the *Raw Power* period are documented in the liner notes to the 2005 *Heavy Liquid* box set released by Easy Action:

There was mess piled upon mess waiting for the release of that record. No one knew how to handle it or the band. The music didn't fit into any recognisable category and the Stooges were speaking in tongues. I became very unsound. I was on a mission basically to destroy the world. By the time the record came out, management and the record company had basically washed their hands of us. I had a band and it had gone to hell.

Post-album release, the band gigged on. Initially, for one performance only on 15 June 1973, the sacked James Williamson was replaced by one Tornado Turner, but a poor band performance resulted in the prompt return of James! The band then finally undertook some more regular gigging from mid-1973 through to February 1974. Scott Thurston replaced Bob Sheff on keyboards around July. The band also continued writing/rehearsing new material for a new album that never happened (although the new songs, such as 'Heavy Liquid', 'Open Up And Bleed', 'I Got Nothing', 'Rich Bitch', 'Rubber Legs', would get live outings). With the band in the firm grip of drink and drugs, they stumbled on as the quality of gigs deteriorated with rapidly diminishing audiences. Things finally came to an end on 9 February 1974 at the Michigan Palace when the band played their last gig (at that time) to a particularly hostile crowd, who famously hurled various projectiles at the poor band onstage – bottles, glasses, coins, cigarettes, ice and eggs. (This infamous gig was later released as the *Metallic KO* LP in 1976, which will be discussed later in the Further Related And Recommended Albums And Songs section.) In early 1974, Columbia also finally gave up on the band. So, after several years of flop albums, poor reviews, no money, and with various band members physically and mentally spent and drug-addled, that was it for nearly 30 years!

Today, over 50 years after its release, this album, however, has well and truly stood the test of time and its legacy and influence cannot be denied. A completely different beast than the first two Stooges albums, this proto-punk, garage rock offering is also infused with hard rock and heavy metal sensibilities. This more aggressive and ferocious sound is in no small part due to the guitar work of James Williamson. Whilst Ron Asheton's energetic lead guitar style evinced a sense of the blues and psychedelia, James' style was even more raw, savage and hard – more 'punk' if you like. James also co-wrote all eight songs on the album. Iggy, lyrically and vocally, is on fire throughout, delivering odes to an angsty, disillusioned youth with spittle and venom (incidentally, some of the lyrics on *Raw Power* were also inspired by some of Iggy's favourite writers, books and films of the time). Meanwhile, Ron and Scott provide a powerhouse rhythm section. Ron may have felt a little slighted at being seemingly 'demoted' to bass, but the guy who had started out as a bassist still absolutely delivered – his pounding basslines are just sublime.

As with their first two albums, this is another highly influential piece of work that went on to inspire many other genres, including punk, hardcore, heavy metal, garage rock, grunge and alternative rock. Punks like Steve Jones (Sex Pistols), Brian James (The Damned) and Mick Jones (The Clash) were all heavily influenced by the record, as indeed were later rockers like Kurt Cobain (Nirvana), Bobby Gillespie (Primal Scream) and Henry Rollins (Black Flag/Rollins Band). Kurt Cobain even stated that *Raw Power* was his favourite album of all time!

British rock critic Nick Kent summed things up nicely (in his 2010 memoir *Apathy For The Devil*) when he called it 'the greatest, meanest-eyed, coldest-blooded hard rock tour de force ever summoned up in a recording studio.' Meanwhile, Stooge guitarist James Williamson had this to say about the record in the 2010 reissue liner notes:

> Nothing has ever sounded like this record before or since ... I am profoundly appreciative of the acceptance that this album has finally achieved, but I was never in any doubt about its intrinsic contribution to the art of rock 'n' roll music; it just took a while.

This album is probably more proto-punk than the band's first two albums with its more conventionally anthemic hard-rock leanings (whereas the first two albums are arguably more groove-oriented). Is it the most dangerous rock 'n' roll album of all time? Well, yes, it quite possibly is!

As with the previous Stooges albums, this one has also been reissued many times over the years. However, notable reissues include the 1997 Columbia/Legacy release, containing Iggy Pop's album remix (carried out in 1996 in collaboration with Bruce Dickinson and Danny Kadar). Regarding his 1996 remix, Iggy had these things to say on the back cover of the 1997 reissue:

> People kept asking me – musicians, kids I would see – 'Have you ever thought about remixing *Raw Power*?' ... Everything's still in the red; it's a very violent mix. The proof's in the pudding.

Iggy always thought the original (Bowie mix) release literally lacked the 'raw power' that the band exhibited at the time and sounded a little fragile and weedy overall. Then, when the first CD version of *Raw Power* came out, he thought it sounded even worse! Sony subsequently invited him to do a remix (in 1996) and encouraged him to get it sounding just how he wanted, and what Iggy wanted was to get that 'raw power' across in the new mix using the latest (at that time) technology (with the added bonus of more money and time to spend on the project).

Whilst the reaction to Bowie's original mix had been varied at best, the reaction to Iggy's remix was equally mixed. James Williamson claimed it 'sucked'. Bowie also reportedly preferred his own earlier mix. Audiophiles, in general, dislike the digital distortion caused by the loudness. Personally, I think I prefer this mix – it's more balanced and clearer but also more muscular-sounding – at least to my ears.

Another common complaint is that Bowie's mix features mainly Iggy and James on vocals/lead guitar, but Ron and Scott (on bass/drums) are buried in the mix. However, Iggy's 1996 remix helped convince some people that perhaps Bowie's mix had not been that bad after all!

About Bowie's mix, James Williamson had this to say in a 2018 *Classic Rock* article:

> The problem was this was not a Bowie style of music – it wasn't tune-y or anything that he usually does. So I think he didn't really understand the music, and he put a real arty overlay on it. There's been a lot of criticism about it over the years, but you've got to give him credit that nothing sounded like it before or since.

2010 saw the two-disc Legacy Edition reissue via Columbia/Legacy – the first disc contains the original album (in its original Bowie/Pop mix) whilst the second disc contains the terrific Georgia Peaches show (Richards, Atlanta, GA, October 1973 – *Raw Power* tracks mixed with some post-*Raw Power* tracks – with Scott Thurston on piano) plus two other tracks: 'Doojiman' (a *Raw Power* sessions outtake) and 'Head On' (a rehearsal performance taken from CBS Studios rehearsal tape). At the same time, there was also a limited Deluxe Edition made available containing three CDs (discs one and two as per the Legacy two-disc set, disc three containing further rarities, outtakes and alternates from the *Raw Power* era), a DVD (containing a *Raw Power* documentary) and a 7" vinyl single (featuring a reproduction of the Japanese 7" 45 RPM single 'Raw Power' b/w 'Search And Destroy').

2023 saw a 50th-anniversary digital release via Columbia/Legacy featuring 34 tracks – the original Bowie/Pop mix remastered, Iggy Pop's 1996 remix remastered, the Georgia Peaches live show and several other bonus tracks, including outtakes from previous Deluxe/Legacy Editions, plus a couple of additional alternate Iggy mixes and a remix.

A James Williamson quote from a 2018 *Classic Rock* article ultimately sums up this album admirably: 'The songs on that album have survived multiple/dubious mixes, the test of time – everything. They still rock, and people still like them ... What else can you say? I think that's a testimony to the songs.'

'Search And Destroy' (Pop, Williamson)

A frenetic guitar and drum intro opens the album up in style, with some sizzling lead guitar work from James Williamson in particular. Iggy's vocals then blast off, sounding better than ever. This is an infectiously rousing and high-energy tune with sterling rhythm support from the Asheton brothers, Ron and Scott. James's blistering guitar helps motor this furious-sounding rocker along at a relentless breakneck speed. Scott's powerhouse drumming should not be overlooked either; he is absolutely on fire here. This tune certainly provides a truly glorious start to the album. Viciously aggressive and filled to the brim with attitude, this is a classic rock 'n' roll tune.

Lyrically, this song is also incredibly rich and visual. The opening lyrics are particularly distinctive: 'I'm a streetwalking cheetah with a heart full of napalm/I'm a runaway son of the nuclear A-bomb/I am a world's forgotten boy/The one who searches and destroys'. Iggy used to wear a cheetah jacket around London at this time and the napalm bit essentially equates to Iggy's anger and frustration at the world around him at the time.

The title of the track came from the headline of an article in *Time* magazine concerning the US war on drugs at the time, whilst some of the other lyrical content was also inspired by the search and destroy missions of the Vietnam War.

The song's classic riff had initially been worked up at RG Jones Studio (in Wimbledon) earlier in the year (apparently, during a break in rehearsals, James started messing around making machine gun sounds with his guitar, which was how the riff originated).

Considered by Iggy to be the record's masterpiece, this song has been covered by a variety of artists, including Red Hot Chili Peppers. Their version was used as a B-side but was also included on some various artists compilations, including the Iggy Pop tribute album *We Will Fall*.

The track was also issued as a single in the US in June 1973 backed with fellow album track 'Penetration'.

'Gimme Danger' (Pop, Williamson)

A slower, moodier tempo beckons on this next tune (as per the record label's request for two ballad-style numbers, one for each side of the record) about Iggy's tendency to opt for girlfriends who would give him trouble. It is certainly more acoustic-flavoured and emits an almost Doors-ish vibe at times, especially with regard to Iggy's vocal croon, which is quite Morrison-esque. An appealingly dark atmosphere pervades the entire piece with a haunting, almost menacing, quality on display throughout, instigated by James' acoustic strumming. Characterful tambourine sounds (and other percussion instruments) in the background help embellish the musical proceedings. There is some rather nice electric lead guitar work during the second half of the track, too. Iggy also lends his piano-playing skills throughout. All in all, it is a bit of a dark masterpiece with echoes and shades of both the Stones and The Doors.

An alternate 1996 Iggy remix of the track was also made available on the limited edition 2010 Deluxe album reissue as a bonus track.

'Your Pretty Face Is Going To Hell' (Originally titled 'Hard To Beat') (Pop, Williamson)
A raucous guitar and drum opening heralds an Iggy cry of 'Alright!' to open this ode to one of the aforementioned troublesome girlfriends. More vocal whooping then ensues before the track is properly off and running. Some relentless riffing from James Williamson then proceeds to propel the song forward. Indeed, James' guitar work is frenzied and energetic throughout, whilst Scott's brutal drumming is also phenomenal. Meanwhile, Iggy's growling and animalistic vocal styling provide a bit of variety (Iggy also plays tambourine here). According to Iggy, the riff is basically James Williamson updating the classic Rolling Stones guitar sound, although a Chuck Berry influence is fairly obvious, too. Uncompromising in nature, this delightfully exuberant rocker also exhibits a bit of a glam strut that was de rigueur at the time.

A rough mix of 'Hard To Beat' (the song's original title), recorded in London in 1972, was made available on the *Extended Play* release from Easy Action in 2005.

An alternate 1996 Iggy remix of the track was also made available on the limited edition 2010 Deluxe reissue of the album as a bonus track.

'Penetration' (Pop, Williamson)
A less boisterous opening this time around as the guitar/drum instrumentation gives way to a snarling, menacing and intense (and echoey) vocal effort from Iggy. Additionally, Iggy also throws in some weird and characterful vocal sounds throughout, best described as deranged caterwauling. Listeners are also treated to some effectively flavoursome backing vocals (from Ron and James), which add harmonic lustre to the tune. Some nice, searing lead guitar sounds from James decorate the second half of the song, whilst some colourful celesta work (courtesy of Iggy) elevates the musical proceedings (indeed, the repetitive celesta line that runs throughout adds a nice haunting, hypnotic quality to the piece). Dark, sensual and exciting, this is fab stuff!

Purportedly, this was the first track Iggy and James really worked on, paving the way for the *Raw Power* album (indeed, Williamson apparently came up with the initial riff idea circa the second half of 1971).

An early version of 'Penetration' from the 1972 London studio sessions is also available on the 2017 *Heavy Liquid* album (released via the Easy Action label and discussed in greater detail later on), which features more prominent use of the backing vocals. Although, in general, it is a looser version, it still sounds very cool.

'Raw Power' (Pop, Williamson)
A lively guitar, drum and piano intro ushers in the album's title track before Iggy's characterful vocals start up and he delivers the great opening line, 'Dance to the beat of the living dead'. This is yet another high-energy rock 'n' roll tune driven by guitar and piano, featuring terrific band member performances all around. Of particular note, Iggy's vocals are absolutely stellar on this one, full of vim and vigour, whilst James' sterling lead guitar work is also worthy of a special mention, exhibiting proto-punk exuberance. Iggy also plays piano and tambourine on this number and provides the backing vocals together with Ron. This relentlessly paced rocker eventually concludes in suitably frantic style – it's awesome and exciting stuff!

The song was released as a single in Japan, backed with fellow album track 'Search And Destroy'. This swaggering, Stones-ish rock 'n' roll tune was also used to open the band's live sets in 1973.

Various artists have covered this classic tune. Notably, Guns N' Roses covered it on their *The Spaghetti Incident?* LP.

'I Need Somebody' (Pop, Williamson)
A bluesy, acoustic-based intro with Iggy yelping in the background helps initiate this next number, ballad number two. Here, we are once again treated to a terrific Iggy vocal display – a sexy, bluesy rock croon full of character. The basic tune is blues-based but delivered here with a darkly romantic ambience. The acoustic/electric guitar interplay throughout is a particular highlight. Another exciting fusion of howling lead guitar sounds and crooning vocals, backed again by some robust rhythmic support from both Scott and Ron, sees the song fade out to a stylish close.

'Shake Appeal' (Pop, Williamson)
Another frenetic instrumental intro, accompanied by some vigorous hand clapping, launches this next track before Iggy's vocal commences, full of vibrancy. This is another high-energy and effervescent tune – a glorious guitar and hand-clap-driven rocker. It is a fairly simple tune in terms of actual musicality, but nonetheless, it still proffers a highly engaging listen with a 1950s rock 'n' roll vibe. Some nice lead guitar soloing from James and a very exuberant vocal display from Iggy throughout help elevate this track.

According to Iggy in *Uncut* in 2023, this is his personal favourite track from the album 'Because that was the only three minutes of my life when I was ever going to approximate Little Richard.'

An early version of 'Shake Appeal', recorded in London in July 1972 (at Olympic Studios) and entitled 'Tight Pants', appears on various releases, such as the *Heavy Liquid* and *Born In A Trailer* box sets (detailed later in the Further Related And Recommended Albums And Songs section). This early version is also highly energetic in nature and has a superfast pace. As with the later finalised version, this track is an extremely vibrant rocker driven by frenzied lead guitar and hand claps.

An alternate mix of 'Shake Appeal' can also be found on the limited edition 2010 Deluxe reissue of the album.

'Death Trip' (Pop, Williamson)
Another raucous guitar/vocal intro opens this closing number, all scorching and screeching guitar sounds and screaming vocal sounds. Iggy turns in yet another spirited vocal performance whilst James' exciting lead guitar sounds also abound once again as he weaves licks and fills throughout the piece. Meanwhile, Ron's bass and Scott's drums attempt to maintain control in the background, with Scott, in particular, furiously thrashing his drum skins throughout. Thrilling and intense, and full of energetic and fully committed performances all around, this near-six-minute epic makes for a suitably great album closer. 'We're going down in history' indeed, as Iggy sings during the song. A furious instrumental and vocal cacophony finally sees the song, and indeed the album, out in a suitably exciting and exhilarating fashion.

Lyrically and thematically, Iggy was apparently singing about the band's career at this juncture – he knew the album was doomed and would likely bomb, that the band's relationship with MainMan was also doomed and that the band would likely come to an end sooner rather than later – this was his attempt at putting all these thoughts into a song!

An alternate mix of the track was also issued on the limited edition 2010 Deluxe reissue of the album as a bonus track.

Other Contemporary Songs
'Doojiman' (Pop, Williamson)
Some relentless drum and bass work powers this outtake, with various improvised vocal sounds coming courtesy of Iggy throughout the piece. Fast-paced and full of energy, James Williamson throws in some rather nice stabs of lead guitar throughout. It is not exactly a proper song as such, but rather, it is just a thoroughly good band workout in the studio.

This track was made available as a bonus track on the 2010 Legacy/Deluxe reissues of the album.

'Head On' (Pop, Williamson)
This rehearsal performance track (recorded in 1973 from a CBS Studios rehearsal tape) makes for a fast-paced, up-tempo rocker. The tune boasts some great full-band instrumentation, including some wonderful tinkling

piano sounds throughout (courtesy of Scott Thurston). Overall, it is an entertaining and appealing tune, full of energy, with the band on fine form. This exciting and powerful rock 'n' roller was often played live during the 1973/74 period. This track is also sometimes known as 'Head On The Curb' and 'Head On Curve'.

This particular rehearsal version of the track appeared as a bonus track on the 2010 Legacy/Deluxe reissues of the album, although various other versions of the song have been issued on a variety of other Stooges-related releases.

'I'm Hungry' (Pop, Williamson)
Another dynamic guitar and drum intro opens this tune, followed by Iggy's shouts of 'I'm Hungry!' We are then off and running with this embryonic (and faster) version of 'Penetration'. The full-on instrumentation continues apace, driven by James' riff work, whilst Iggy throws in random vocal sounds and improvised lyrics regarding food and hunger. Up-tempo and high energy throughout, this *Raw Power* outtake is a fun listen.

This track appeared as a bonus track on the 2010 Deluxe reissue of the album.

'I Got A Right' (sometimes credited to Pop, Williamson but also to Pop alone)
This track begins with a guitar/drum intro, which quickly leads into a frenzied full-band musical onslaught delivered at a frantic pace. The tune boasts some raw and energetic vocals from Iggy (raging about his rights!), great soloing from James and fantastic rhythm support from Ron and Scott Asheton. This tune is a terrific punk rocker before punk was even a thing!

This dynamic number was part of the band's live set (in 1971) prior to attempts at recording it in the studio (July 1972). For some reason, the band left the track behind when it came to the proper *Raw Power* album sessions in September/October 1972. Perhaps they were simply bored of it by this time.

This particular version of the outtake appeared as a bonus track on the 2010 Deluxe reissue of the album, although various other versions of the track have appeared on a number of Stooges-related releases over the years. This song was also released as a single in 1977.

'I'm Sick Of You' (Pop, Williamson)
A sombre instrumental opening ensues before Iggy begins his sinister-sounding vocals. This period of solemnity plays out over the first two-and-a-half minutes before the tempo is upped during the mid-part of the song, where we are treated to some blazing lead guitar sounds from James that is redolent of The Yardbirds' 'Happenings Ten Years Time Ago'. The tempo slows again for the latter part of the song, with the track coming to a gradual climax close to the seven-minute mark.

This outtake, from an early aborted *Raw Power* session, appears on the 2010 Deluxe reissue of the album. Also, despite being unreleased back in the day, it was subsequently included on many other Stooges-related releases issued over the years. Indeed, it was also released as early as 1977 when it was issued as a single.

'Hey, Peter' (Pop, Williamson)
Hard-hitting drum beats and spirited guitar sounds provide the backup on this one to some Iggy-improvised lyrics. This is an up-tempo and energetic rocker, which is interesting to hear as a fan but, ultimately, inconsequential in nature.

This *Raw Power* outtake appeared on the 2010 Deluxe reissue of the album.

'Gimme Some Skin' (Pop, Williamson)
This is an extremely lively, punky tune from the off, featuring a hyperactive vocal display from Iggy and further frantic lead guitar work from James. Scott Asheton manages to hold things together (just!) on drums. This is another highly energetic and engaging tune; at under three minutes in length, it's short and sweet.

This pre-*Raw Power* track was worked on by the band at Olympic Studios in London in July 1972 and, despite being unreleased at the time, has subsequently been made available on a variety of Stooges-related releases over the years. This outtake was also released on a single in 1977.

'Louie Louie' (Berry)
This is a fun and entertaining band run-through of this old classic rock 'n' roll tune (which starts with a sample of The Trashmen's 'Surfin' Bird'). The take of this loose workout was recorded during the July 1972 sessions held at Olympic Studios and has been made available on a variety of Stooges releases over the years.

'Money' (Gordy, Bradford)
Another cover version (this time of the Gordy/Bradford rhythm and blues classic) but not as good as the 'Louie Louie' run-through. This is an even looser and more ragged band workout. It is interesting to listen to as a fan, but there is nothing particularly special to be found here.

This take was also recorded during the July 1972 sessions held at Olympic Studios. Again, it has been readily available on a variety of Stooges releases over the years.

'Scene Of The Crime' (Pop, Williamson)
This is a guitar-driven rocker featuring a raucous Iggy vocal performance. Some characterful piano adds flavour to the rock instrumentation, but this remains a relentlessly paced number. It also features some great drumming from Scott Asheton. Overall, another vibrant and 'punky' band performance.

This track was also worked on by the band at Olympic Studios in London in July 1972 and, again, despite being unreleased at the time, has subsequently been made available on a number of Stooges releases over the years. Indeed, it was also included on a single release as early as 1977.

'Instrumental' (Pop, Williamson)
Available on Easy Action's 2017 *Heavy Liquid* release (discussed later in greater depth), this is a cool-sounding, up-tempo and spirited rock workout with the band members getting to flex their respective musical muscles. A fun-sounding romp that was recorded in London in 1972.

Post-Break-Up/Reunion

After the breakup, Iggy, whilst still in the grip of drug addiction, briefly worked with The Doors' Ray Manzarek, but, ultimately, nothing substantial came of this pairing and it wasn't too long before Iggy's ravaged mental and physical health led him to a psychiatric unit (circa autumn 1974). A few people visited Iggy and stayed in touch – one of these visitors was ex-Stooge James Williamson. Iggy and James subsequently started writing songs together again, and eventually, some demos were recorded (circa 1975, with a view to obtaining a new record deal). James oversaw the sessions with Iggy recording his vocals whilst on day release from the psych unit. Maybe unsurprisingly, given Iggy's notoriety at the time, no record companies were interested in signing the pair and the songs went unreleased for a while. However, a couple of years further down the line, in 1977, these songs did eventually see the light of day when they were released via Bomp! as the *Kill City* LP (see the later Further Related And Recommended Albums And Songs section for further details).

Another rare visitor for Iggy was David Bowie. They started hanging out and, reportedly, started working on new material together. This friendship eventually led to Iggy being invited to accompany Bowie on his *Station To Station* tour in early 1976 (with a view to the pair recording an album together once the touring had been completed).

Indeed, the pair spent the best part of the next 18 months together, eventually moving to Europe and recording two classic solo Iggy albums – *The Idiot* (UK number 30/US number 72) and *Lust For Life* (UK number 28) – which proved to be Iggy's first real commercial successes. Once Iggy's solo career had been established, with assistance from the Thin White Duke, he proceeded to release a number of solo albums over the next three decades and toured relentlessly. He even began acting, too, in the mid-1980s, appearing in a succession of movies and TV shows. By the 1990s, he had essentially become a bona fide rock star and mainstream celebrity, with his music and imagery appearing regularly in adverts, films and TV shows.

James Williamson ended up producing Iggy's *New Values* LP (1979) and also started producing its follow-up LP, *Soldier* (1980), before a falling out led to him being replaced. James then decided to leave the music biz and started a career in the electronics industry, eventually resulting in a Silicon Valley career (until a reunion with the Stooges in 2009).

Post-Stooges, Ron Asheton went on to play with a number of bands – The New Order (with ex-Stooges Jimmy Recca and Scott Thurston), Destroy All Monsters, New Race and Dark Carnival – and even became a B-movie actor at one point.

His brother Scott, meanwhile, initially joined Sonic's Rendezvous Band (started by Fred 'Sonic' Smith, ex-MC5; SRB also ended up backing Iggy on his 1978 European tour) before being kept busy by a number of other regular music jobs.

Original Stooge bassist Dave Alexander sadly died in February 1975 from pulmonary oedema brought on by pancreatitis (which was most likely linked to his alcohol abuse). He was aged just 27.

Circa 1976/77, a few years after the band breakup, the punk movement well and truly arrived, and with it, the Stooges' legacy as punk pioneers (and, indeed, Iggy's legacy as the 'godfather of punk') began in earnest. The Stooges' live LP *Metallic KO* arrived in 1976, closely followed by a handful of singles in 1977 (as mentioned previously, the live record contained recordings from the band's riotous last gig in February 1974, whilst the singles contained the previously unreleased pre-*Raw Power* tracks). These were all well received by the punk community, and the British music press (the likes of *NME*, *Sounds*, etc.) even began to champion Iggy and the band. Many of the new kids on the block (Sex Pistols, The Damned, etc.) also began to cite Iggy and The Stooges as big influences. Joy Division's Peter Hook was also a big fan of *Metallic KO*.

The band's legacy and influence continued to grow, and throughout the 1980s, US alternative rock/punk/grunge bands started to spring up – the likes of Jane's Addiction, Sonic Youth, Pixies, Red Hot Chili Peppers, Nirvana, etc., and they all namechecked Iggy and The Stooges. US rocker Henry Rollins is another famously huge fan of the band. Indeed, over the ensuing decades, alt-rockers, grunge rockers and even metal acts have all been happy to cite Iggy and Co. as major influences on them.

Whilst their legacy grew, there was intermittent talk about a band reunion. Scott Asheton apparently approached Iggy as early as the late 1980s regarding a Stooges reunion, but Iggy reportedly said it was not the right time. There was also some further talk circa the mid-1990s about a possible reunion (talk between Ron Asheton and Iggy this time), but timing proved to be an issue for both of them, respectively, and a proposed late 1990s reunion never happened.

In 1998, Ron Asheton found himself recruited as part of supergroup Wylde Ratttz (together with Sonic Youth's Thurston Moore and Steve Shelley, Mudhoney's Mark Arm and ex-Minutemen and fIREHOSE bassist Mike Watt). The band was put together to record some music for Todd Haynes' glam rock tribute movie *Velvet Goldmine*, which was very loosely based on the relationship between Iggy Pop and David Bowie. The band initially recorded several Stooges covers and a couple of original numbers, although only a recording of 'T.V. Eye' ended up on the film soundtrack, with vocals provided by actor Ewan McGregor (who plays the Iggy-like character Curt Wild in the movie). Another song (an original, 'My Unclean') also appeared in the movie itself, but that was it. The group also went on to record some further original music as well as some other covers a short while later, but this did not see the light of day until it was released digitally in 2020.

By early 2001, J Mascis (from Dinosaur Jr.) and Mike Watt were touring with Mascis' The Fog when Ron Asheton began joining them on some of the dates. The Fog had been performing a couple of Stooges songs in their set, so when they visited Ron's hometown on tour, they thought it would be fun to get the original Stooges guitarist up on stage with them to perform those numbers. Things went so well that Ron joined them for further dates and they ended up playing several other Stooges songs at these shows. A little later, brother Scott joined, thus eventually leading to a supergroup of J Mascis, Mike Watt and both Asheton brothers – billed as Asheton, Asheton, Mascis and Watt – who then went on to perform further gigs playing Stooges numbers.

Around the same time, Iggy was preparing his next solo LP (which would become the *Skull Ring* LP – an album of collaborations with young, of-the-moment punks such as Sum 41 and Green Day). However, Iggy got wind of the Ashetons touring and playing Stooges songs, which got him thinking! Subsequently, Iggy got in touch with Ron with regards to him and Scott playing on Iggy's new album. Iggy detailed his thoughts in the *Escaped Maniacs* DVD liner notes:

What really changed things was that I was out on tour for *Beat 'Em Up* (2001) and I heard everywhere I went, 'Hey, Ron's out on tour with Dinosaur Jr. doing Stooges songs and it's real good.' Or I was in Europe and I'd hear, 'Ron and Scott are both out with Mike Watt doing Stooges songs at festivals.' And I thought, whoa, they're out there playing the material, so that kind of raised my eyebrows a little bit.

The Asheton's readily accepted Iggy's invitation and, therefore, early in 2003, undertook recording sessions with Iggy, resulting in four new tracks for his *Skull Ring* album (written by the trio and produced by Iggy). News of this Stooges reunion soon spread, and the guys got invited to play (as the reformed Stooges) at the 2003 Coachella Festival. The trio accepted the invitation and soon recruited recent pal Mike Watt (bass) and old pal Steve Mackay (sax) in order to complete the new lineup. On 27 April 2003, the reformed Stooges played to an audience of around 30,000 people at Coachella and were hailed as conquering heroes! Neil Strauss from The New York Times said of the Coachella performance:

As Mr Pop yowled through a fierce, rumbling version of 'T.V. Eye', it was more than clear that in the 33 years since the song was recorded, the genre has largely been variations on a theme. And the first two Stooges albums are the theme.

Post-Coachella, the reunion became permanent and Iggy's record company at the time (Virgin) were very excited by its promise (as indeed was the rest of the music industry) and wanted a whole new Stooges album. Before that happened, though, the band continued touring to large and ecstatic crowds, with the group performing better than ever before. A big homecoming gig in Detroit was planned for 14 August 2003 (at the DTE Energy Music Theatre), but due to regional power cuts, it was rescheduled for 11 days later. Again, the band were treated like conquering heroes, very different from the way they were treated back in early 1974, just before they folded.

Iggy's *Skull Ring* LP finally arrived in September 2003 in the UK and in November 2003 in the US, receiving mixed to positive reviews, although I think it is fair to say that the positivity was mainly focussed on the Stooges reunion tracks. The four tracks in question (featuring Iggy, Ron – who covered both guitar and bass – and Scott) include:

'Little Electric Chair' (Pop, Asheton, Asheton)
A feisty guitar and drum intro explodes out of the speakers and is soon joined by Iggy's whooping vocals and characteristic hand claps. Iggy's lead vocal then starts up properly and he delivers a quite youthful-sounding and snidey vocal. There is a decent and reliably distorted riff throughout courtesy of Ron and a reasonably catchy chorus, which finds Iggy breezily informing us that 'They'll be fryin' up your hair/In that little electric chair'! Scott's drumming remains basic but incredibly loud and powerful, whilst Ron's guitar licks throughout and solo at the end are also very entertaining. This relentlessly-paced tune is packed full of energy and makes for a fun and vigorous comeback tune.

'Skull Ring' (Pop, Asheton, Asheton)
Another dynamic and colourful guitar/drum beginning introduces the second Stooges number on the album. Iggy's vocals then commence and we are off and running. This more mid-tempo number features an appealing and repetitive 'Peter Gunn'-esque riff from Ron and there is even a brief blast of some trademark wah-wah guitar action from him during the latter part of the song. Iggy, meanwhile, delivers a suitably sardonic vocal turn, repeatedly reminding listeners of his priorities in life: 'Skull rings/Fast cars/Hot chicks/Money'. Overall, this is another pleasingly entertaining listen and a cool tune.

'Loser' (Pop, Asheton, Asheton)
With another dynamic guitar/drum instrumental opening and an Iggy call of 'Alright', this is just like old times. A fairly catchy and decently paced rocker, this again features a colourful and characteristic vocal effort from Iggy, albeit it sounds a little overly self-conscious at times. More insistent riffing from Ron drives the song along throughout, whilst Scott provides the jackhammer drum beats. There is also some more impressive wah-wah soloing from Ron during the latter part of the song, which is always welcome. It's not as good as the previous two numbers, in my humble opinion, but it's still perfectly listenable.

'Dead Rock Star' (Pop, Asheton, Asheton)
More wah-wah guitar sounds, backed by crashing drums and Iggy's 'woo-ooh's, initiate this final Stooges number on Iggy's *Skull Ring* LP. Ron's

delightfully insistent riff then erupts, and we are off again. Iggy delivers a nice, crooning, almost Bowie-esque vocal on this one and the lyrics are effectively world-weary and downbeat ('What can I hope for?/Nothing to live for/I'm a dead rock star'). The chorus is pretty catchy, but it's the very charming and attractive melodic verses that truly elevate the proceedings, which helps make it my favourite of the *Skull Ring* bunch.

In 2005, a tribute album for juke joint blues legend Junior Kimbrough, entitled *Sunday Nights: The Songs Of Junior Kimbrough*, was released on the Fat Possum label (recorded in 2004) and included a contribution from the then recently reformed Iggy and The Stooges. The band perform Kimbrough's 'You Better Run' (in fact, the album actually contains two different versions of this track by the band) – the band kickstart the tune with some blistering instrumentation before Iggy commences his colourful vocal, which is delivered in a typically raw and unhinged style. The band then continue to deliver a frenzied instrumental onslaught, barely staying in control of their instruments. Crunchy riffs, frantic fills and madcap drum beats are the order of the day on this energetic and fast-paced rocker. Overall, it's an engaging band performance full of passion and vigour. Ultimately, it stands up as a fine tribute to the American blues musician. The second version of the song on the tribute album is a slower, bluesier take that runs almost two minutes longer.

The Weirdness (2007)

Personnel:
Iggy Pop: vocals
Ron Asheton: guitar
Scott Asheton: drums
Mike Watt: bass
Additional musicians:
Steve Mackay: sax
Brendan Benson: harmony vocals on 'Free & Freaky'
Recorded at Electrical Audio Studios, Chicago, Illinois, US (October 2006)
Recorded by Steve Albini
UK release date: March 2007
US release date: March 2007
Chart places: UK: 81, US: 130

The reunited band continued touring on and off for the next three years (to rapturous global crowds) before finally hitting the studios in the autumn of 2006 to record *The Weirdness* (as mentioned earlier, there had been record label interest in a new Stooges album almost immediately after the initial *Skull Ring* reunion tracks, but the band wanted to take their time in putting a new album together). Ron apparently wanted the band to produce the record themselves, but Iggy thought an external voice would be more beneficial. Therefore, when the band entered Electrical Audio Studios (Chicago), a certain Steve Albini (who had worked with the Pixies and Nirvana) was present to help record the new record. By all accounts, a good working relationship was established in the studio, with the group aim being for a 'live' feel to the new record, with minimal overdubs.

The completed album was released (via Virgin) in March 2007 and was followed by a major world tour. Sadly and disappointingly, the album met with mixed reviews at best, generally leaning more towards the negative end of the spectrum. On the plus side, the accompanying tour was warmly received (readers are advised to check out the *Telluric Chaos* CD, released on Skydog in 2005, or the *Live In Detroit* DVD for evidence of their supreme live prowess at the time).

Uncut magazine gave it a one-star review and concluded that '*The Weirdness* is like Woody Allen romancing Julia Roberts in *Everyone Says I Love You*. It ain't too believable, and it ain't gonna win any Oscars. And you want to look away.' *Rolling Stone* was more generous in its review: 'Like all reunion albums, it's a flier for the live show, and the point is to hear the Asheton brothers bring it. Scott's drums remain the band's most overlooked strength, and Ron stomps his wah-wah pedal as if he caught it keying his car.'

Overall, the LP presents very spirited and dynamic instrumental performances by Ron and Scott, but sadly, a lot of the tempos are identical, and many of the melodies/choruses are similarly unmemorable. A big weakness of the album is Iggy himself. His lyrics are pretty feeble at times and his vocal delivery is mostly fairly poor (especially when compared with earlier works). There are a few tracks that offer a nice, appealing change of pace and a few of the rockier and faster-paced numbers proffer decent enough listens. However, disappointingly, the majority of tracks on the record generally follow the same musical template of fast-paced instrumental noise backing repetitious and inane lyrics. One strength of the album, however, is Steve Mackay's guest sax work. This is ironic, given my general dislike of his work on the *Fun House* LP, but here, his sax sounds do add some much-needed colour to the musical proceedings.

Ultimately, the record stalled at number 130 on the US album charts and number 81 on the UK charts. With a final production mix that is a tad muddy and dull, the new studio album not only failed to capture the magic of their first three albums but also failed in its attempt to capture the sound and energy of their comeback shows. Critics, quite rightly, took a potshot at Iggy's rather cringeworthy lyrics, and, as mentioned earlier, it did not help matters that Iggy's vocal quality was also a little off on this record. Also, although still incredibly noisy and forceful, Ron's guitar work and Scott's drumming lack some of that early trademark primal groove. Although the album opens with a decent rocker, it sadly soon dissolves into an undistinguishable mush of uninspired riffs and vapid choruses, barring a few exceptions. Therefore, in conclusion, there is some good stuff to be found on the album; there is just simply not anywhere near enough!

'Trollin" (Pop, Asheton, Asheton)

A full-on band cacophony of guitar, drum and vocal sounds helps launch this first number, which serves as a suitably boisterous album-opening track. Featuring lively and energetic instrumentation throughout, the sound here is attractively rambunctious. Sadly, Iggy proceeds to let this one down ever so slightly. His vocals sound a little buried in the mix (although to be honest, the whole production sounds a little muddy) and the lyrical content is a little on the weak side. An example of the highbrow lyrics on display here include the classy 'My dick is turning into a tree!', which doesn't exactly bode well for the rest of the album! Ron, however, delivers a muscular riff and colourful licks whilst Scott's drumming is suitably sinewy. So, all in all, it is a fairly fun, up-tempo and vigorous tune to start the album with, even if it's not exactly what you would call a classic.

'You Can't Have Friends' (Pop, Asheton, Asheton)

This is another high-energy guitar and drum-driven rocker with Ron on trademark wah-wah duty and Scott again on fine form (Albini's production adds bite to both brothers' instruments). Sadly, Iggy's vocals and lyrics are even weaker here than on the previous number, and it is not exactly a memorable melody either. Iggy bores listeners with the repetitive rhyming couplet 'I wanna be your friend/Until the bitter end' with a strange, strained-sounding vocal delivery. Luckily, it is only just over two minutes in length, so it's all over before too long.

'ATM' (Pop, Asheton, Asheton)
Another vibrant and dynamic guitar/drum intro initiates this next rocker, which closely follows the musical template already firmly established by the opening two tracks. Again, it is hardly a memorable or original-sounding tune, but the energy levels are at least kept high throughout. Disappointingly, Iggy's vocals and lyrics (referencing his personal wealth) yet again provide the weakest link here, whilst Ron, Scott and Mike are left to do their best to elevate the proceedings with their slightly unruly and live-sounding instrumentation.

This was reportedly a later written number when the band knew they had to get the album's writing done and dusted and, sadly, it shows!

'My Idea Of Fun' (Pop, Asheton, Asheton)
Yet again, we are here presented with another energetic and up-tempo rocker but without a standout melody or appealing chorus to elevate it. Iggy's vocal performance also disappoints again as he struggles to hit all the necessary notes whilst he spends most of his time repeating the phrase, 'My idea of fun is killing everyone!' On the plus side, Albini's production helps the instrumentation sound full and noisy throughout. Ron delivers a blistering guitar solo during the latter part of the song, whilst Scott frantically thrashes his drum skins.

This track was actually released as a promo single and was reportedly one of the earlier numbers to be written by the reunited band.

'The Weirdness' (Pop, Asheton, Asheton)
Finally, we are treated to a change of pace and tempo with the album's title track. Iggy charmingly croons away, sounding better here than on the previous four tracks, whilst Ron offers some bluesy lead guitar sounds throughout. Scott, meanwhile, provides a solid yet relatively subtle background beat. Sax sounds enter the picture during the second half of the song, courtesy of Steve Mackay, adding a complementary flavour to the musical proceedings (which differs from the old *Fun House* days when Mackay's contributions tended to be more of a disruptive influence on the band's music). This is a decent enough tune, even if it is not exactly a masterpiece.

Interestingly, Iggy was apparently proud of this gentler, moodier tune because he felt it showed growth within the band.

'Free & Freaky' (Pop, Asheton, Asheton)
Disappointingly, on this next tune, we find ourselves back in the all too

familiar comfort zone of up-tempo, high-energy sounds. Boisterous rock instrumentation backs Iggy on another lyrically weak number. 'Free and freaky in the USA' is the oft-repeated phrase on display here, whilst other lyrical delights include:

England and France
These cultures are old
The cheese is stinky
And the beer ain't cold
When I go over there I gotta walk bold

Iggy delivers these disposable lines in an equally throwaway fashion, leaving the rest of the band to pick up the slack again. Ron throws in a decent riff and some lively licks whilst Scott also commits full-bloodedly to the task at hand. Sadly, Mike Watt's bass is a little lost in the mix, but I'm sure he's pulling his weight! Thankfully, the song does not outstay its welcome and ceases just over the two-and-a-half-minute mark.
This number was also released as a promo single.

'Greedy Awful People' (Pop, Asheton, Asheton)
More of the same on this next number. Dynamic guitar and drum sounds drive things along at exactly the same pace and tempo as all the previous rockers, essentially leaving listeners feeling as though they've already heard this track before! This is another pretty lame and disposable effort from Iggy, with the other band members again left attempting to compensate. Ron, Scott and Mike, therefore, do their best to inject some life into it with their committed instrumental performances, with Ron, in particular, delivering a sizzling wah-wah-infused guitar solo during the second half of the song. It is hard to get past the poor vocals and lyrics, though ('I can't live among my class/I'm thinking only baby about scoring your piece of ass')! Thankfully, this tune again barely breaks the two-minute barrier, so it is all over and done with quickly!

'She Took My Money' (Pop, Asheton, Asheton)
Yet another similar tempo beckons on this next rocker, and it is really just more of the same. Ron, Scott and Mike power away instrumentally, making a lively, if forgettable, noise, while Iggy turns in another slightly below-par vocal effort with lots of repetition of the song's title. Again, I suppose it is an okay listen, but there is just nothing that memorable on display here. The drumming is a little workmanlike and the riff is a little perfunctory, although some of Ron's licks liven things up a bit in places. The addition of Steve Mackay's sax, however, during the last third of the track does add some much-needed complementary colour to the musical proceedings, with some attractive jazzy licks on display.

'The End Of Christianity' (Pop, Asheton, Asheton)

More urgent and insistent guitar/drum sounds kickstart this following number before Iggy's vocals soon start up and listeners must endure another case of déjà vu! Lively, energetic, yet unmemorable instrumentation pounds away in the background whilst Iggy struggles to hit the notes. The lyrics mainly consist of the song's title being repeated. So, just more of the same really!

'Mexican Guy' (Pop, Asheton, Asheton)

Thankfully, this next tune offers some variety. There is a more engaging Bo Diddley-esque beat to start with, accompanied by a suitably traditional rock 'n' roll riff from Ron, which is more clearly defined than on previous songs. Iggy's lyrics are entertainingly daft on this effort, too, and he delivers them in a characterful, more committed fashion this time around:

> The brain police are watching my back
> My sanity is under attack
> I've got a crazy look in my eye
> Since my girl ran off with a Mexican guy

Meanwhile, Ron's sizzling lead guitar work during the latter part of the song is a particular highlight as he dazzles listeners with his effervescent soloing.
Reportedly, this was another one of the earliest tunes written for the album.

'Passing Cloud' (Pop, Asheton, Asheton)

Mackay's sax opens this next tune, on which we are treated to another pretty good Iggy vocal turn. Jazzier in feel, owing to Mackay's musical dominance, it offers a nice change of flavour. Ron's wah-wah sounds duelling with Mackay's sax sounds later on is also a particular highlight. Lyrically, it is also one of the more pleasing offerings on the album, with Iggy eschewing the usual crude and crass content for something a little more considered and meditative as he self-reflects. Overall, this is indeed one of the better tracks on the LP with its engaging jazzy dynamics.
This was another later written number for the album.

'I'm Fried' (Pop, Asheton, Asheton)

On the album's closing number, we return to the frantic and frenetic pace of earlier, complete with some rather banal lyrics and lots of repetition of the song's title. Again, there is a lot of energy to the musical proceedings, but it is all just a little unmemorable, sadly. Ron throws in a generic riff and a few tasty licks and is backed by an incredibly noisy rhythm section. Mackay's sax then cuts in during the second half of the song, adding some much-needed colour again via some discordant licks. The song, and indeed the album, then eventually draws to a close, with the band producing a rousing and almighty instrumental cacophony behind Iggy's slightly unhinged vocals.

Other Contemporary Songs

'O Solo Mio' (Pop, Asheton, Asheton)
Heavy, sombre and melancholy, this number features a more thoughtful and introspective lyric as Iggy offers further self-reflection. Slower in tempo, this rather moody and atmospheric tune is, in my humble opinion, a far better offering than most of the other tracks from the main album. Ron plays an enticing melody throughout the piece with sympathetic support from brother Scott on drums. It is a veritable mini-epic, running at just over six minutes in length.

This song was a vinyl edition and Japanese edition-only bonus track.

'Claustrophobia' (Pop, Asheton, Asheton)
A nice frenetic fusion of electric guitar and drum beats opens this one up before Iggy enters the scene with a slightly unhinged vocal performance. There's a pleasing, albeit basic, rock 'n' roll riff from Ron on display, with some additional solo flourishing towards the end. Similarly, Scott's drumming is a tad rudimentary, but you can't fault his energetic enthusiasm. Although this tune ploughs a very similar musical furrow to the majority of songs on the main album (up-tempo, daft lyrics, generic rock riff, basic drum beats), it manages to do so in a much more agreeable manner. As with the previous bonus track, 'O Solo Mio', I think it's better than a lot of the other tracks that were actually released on the main album.

This tune was a vinyl edition-only bonus track.

'I Wanna Be Your Man' (Lennon, McCartney)
This is a fun, highly energetic band run-through of the early Lennon and McCartney classic. It's entertaining and, again, probably more enjoyable than a lot of the other tracks on the main album. It's certainly rawer than The Beatles' take and a lot more raucous; it is probably closer in spirit to The Rolling Stones' 1963 version.

This track was a vinyl edition and iTunes edition-only bonus track.

'Sounds Of Leather' (Pop, Asheton, Asheton)
On display here, we have another crunchy riff, more primal drum sounds and a slightly deadpan vocal performance. Probably the weakest of the bonus tracks here, it again still offers a more interesting listen than most of the songs on the main album. It is a thoroughly decent little rocker, which was a vinyl edition-only bonus track.

Ready To Die (2013)
Personnel:
Iggy Pop: vocals
James Williamson: guitars
Scott Asheton: drums
Mike Watt: bass
Steve Mackay: saxophone
Toby Dammit: percussion (recorded at Candy Bomber Studios, Berlin)
Additional musicians:
Scott Thurston: keyboards on 'Beat That Guy' (recorded at Groove Masters, Santa Monica, CA)
Petra Haden: violin and backing vocals on 'Beat That Guy', backing vocals on 'Sex & Money'
Mark Culbertson: contrabass on 'Beat That Guy'
Don Rooke: electric lap steel on 'The Departed'
Hugh Marsh: violin on 'The Departed'
Michelle Willis: pump organ on 'The Departed'
Jesse Nichols: additional percussion on 'Gun', 'DD's', 'Job', 'Ready To Die' and 'Sex & Money'
Jason Butler: additional percussion on 'Unfriendly World'
Recorded at Fantasy Studios, Berkeley, CA; vocals recorded at South Beach Studios, Miami (except for vocals on 'Job', which were recorded at Studio 606, Northridge, CA)
Produced by James Williamson
UK release date: April 2013
US release date: April 2013
Chart places: UK: 77, US: 96

Sadly, Ron Asheton passed away in January 2009 from a heart attack, but this was not the end of the story. After Ron's death, Iggy contacted James Williamson and invited him to rejoin the band (as mentioned earlier, James had retired from the music industry in the 1980s to pursue a career in the electronics industry. Indeed, he was apparently senior Vice President of technology standards at Sony when he decided to resign/take early retirement and re-enter the music biz). Thus, Iggy and The Stooges were reborn, with the 'Iggy and' prefix back in place (mirroring the band name back in the Williamson lineup/*Raw Power* days).

This reunion was shortly followed by the band's 2010 induction into the Rock and Roll Hall of Fame. The band had actually been nominated several times for the Hall of Fame before this belated induction, which finally saw the Stooges getting the respect they had long deserved.

With James back in the fold, the band carried on touring the world (often performing *Raw Power* in full), with their live shows continuing to be highly energetic, incendiary affairs.

2013 eventually saw the release of a new album with the Williamson lineup (James also produced the new record). The new LP also featured Larry Mullins (aka Toby Dammit) on drum duty. Larry had drummed with Iggy throughout the 1990s, so he was well known to him. Sadly, Scott Asheton's deteriorating health at the time meant that Larry shared drum duties on the record (Larry also replaced Scott for some live shows).

Upon release (via the Fat Possum label), the general critical consensus was that it was a much better reunion album than *The Weirdness* had been, even if, once again, it did not really come close to approaching the brilliance of their original trilogy of albums. *The Guardian* newspaper singled out the album's ballads as its true strength: 'It feels an odd thing to say about a Stooges album, but the best moments are the ballads, which have a power and sincerity lacking elsewhere ... infinitely more potent than all the caricatures of previous glories.' *Allmusic* concluded that '*Ready To Die* is, against all odds, a terrific Stooges album.' *NME* called it 'a fat, satisfying slab of Iggy punk-rock steak.' As a cherry on the cake, the LP peaked at number 96 on the US album charts, which made it their highest-charting LP on the *Billboard* 200.

Certainly, if one approaches the album with the mindset that it will not be quite as good as the original trilogy of Stooges albums, then you will find plenty to enjoy within its ten tracks! It oozes a sleazy sense of fun throughout and James Williamson's presence on the record as co-writer, guitarist and producer lends a pleasing cohesion to proceedings. Nearly 30 years out of the game did nothing to diminish Williamson's thrilling, fiery and dirty-sounding guitar work. Iggy's vocals are also better here than on *The Weirdness* (although still not as good as in his prime; the ravages of time and lifestyle choices, unsurprisingly, left their mark). Although there are still some laughably juvenile and embarrassing moments to be found, Iggy's lyrics have also improved here. The band are generally tight and focused throughout, and Steve Mackay's sax work is pretty effective.

Overall, *Ready To Die* offers a lot of high-energy, exuberant and entertaining rockers, but there are also moments of more mature reflection as evinced by the three slower-paced and acoustic-based tunes found within.

'Burn' (Pop, Williamson)

A frenzied yet compelling instrumental opening featuring some sizzling lead guitar from James Williamson and sterling drum work from Scott initiates this first number. It is a muscular, catchy and up-tempo rock 'n' roll tune, which sets the scene nicely for the rest of the album. Iggy also turns in a full-blooded vocal performance. On this album opener, after nearly three decades out of the game, James shows absolutely no sign of rustiness as his guitar skills positively shine. It's a real thrill to hear him cranking out his multi-layered power chord contributions again. Welcome back, James! Scott also beats his drum kit as if his life depends on it.

This track was quite rightly selected as a promo single for the album.

'Sex & Money' (Pop, Williamson)
A rocking, sax-infused intro signals the start of this next track. Featuring characteristic handclaps and backing vocals throughout, this decently paced rocker also finds Steve Mackay's breezy sax sounds continuing to add colour throughout the piece. Iggy turns in another wry vocal effort, regaling listeners with a tune concerning two of his favourite topics – sex and money. Iggy treats us to such lyrical subtlety as 'Nipples come and nipples go/But evil love goes for the dough'. Although Iggy's lyrical content has always often veered into lecherous territory, the early days would at least see some attempt at coded subtlety. However, at this stage in the game, there are no such attempts.

All in all, though, it is another thoroughly good rock 'n' roller featuring a terrific Williamson guitar performance as he snakes and weaves his way through the spaces left by Iggy and Mackay.

'Job' (Pop, Williamson)
Another nice, lively and energetic instrumental intro (somewhat similar to the intro on their classic *Fun House* track 'Loose') initiates this next number before Iggy's vocals kick in. However, although buoyant, there is a fairly basic rock 'n' roll groove on display here, and it's the least interesting, most generic tune on the album thus far. I am also not sure if Iggy is singing from the point of view of a struggling blue-collar worker or himself as a rock star when he bemoans working hard whilst earning little money – maybe both! Either way, it's really just an average track that offers a mildly entertaining listen, but I don't think it is as good as the first two tracks. However, James continues to shine on the guitar and delivers a livewire solo towards the end of the song as he battles against Iggy's vocals.

'Gun' (Pop, Williamson)
This is yet another up-tempo and spirited rocker, with James treating listeners to some appealing riff work throughout. Indeed, the tune starts with some slashing, multi-tracked chords redolent of the intro to Bowie's 'Suffragette City'. Iggy, meanwhile, informs us that 'If I had a fuckin' gun/I could shoot at everyone'. A not-so-subtle meditation on America's relationship with violence, this entertaining and exuberant rock 'n' roller boasts plenty of punky guitar sounds. Indeed, Williamson delivers intermittent guitar breaks that remind us why most punk groups looked up to him back in the 1970s.

'Unfriendly World' (Pop, Williamson)
There is a welcome change of pace with this next number, which is a more acoustic-flavoured country ballad-style tune. This introspective and more thoughtful piece (with Iggy lamenting on the cruelties of the world) also features a more appropriately nuanced (yet still characterful) vocal from Iggy, who actually turns in a rather decent Leonard Cohen impression. All in all, it

is quietly appealing, with nice, delicate band member performances all around, especially Williamson's considered acoustic work.

'Ready To Die' (Pop, Williamson)
We're back to the regular high-energy rock instrumentation with this next number, the album's title track. It is all perfectly fine, but it lacks a truly killer riff or melody to really set it off. Iggy gets to deliver a fairly depressing lyric, repeatedly informing listeners that he's 'ready to die'. James, meanwhile, lays on a crunchy riff throughout and there's also a nice guitar solo from him towards the end of the song. Furthermore, some attractive percussive (tambourine) sounds add colour to the usual rock instrumentation. The track then rather abruptly comes to an end at just over the three-minute mark.

'DD's' (Pop, Williamson)
Iggy's rather crass ode to large female breasts ('I'm on my knees for those DD's') features some rather dynamic and ebullient instrumentation throughout (led by Steve Mackay's perky sax sounds). The rather embarrassing and cringeworthy lyrics are about as deep and subtle as one would expect from Iggy, given the song's subject matter, and he delivers them in a rather self-conscious fashion. Overall, however, it is a buoyant enough tune with Scott Asheton on fine drumming form here, treating his skins to a fair old bashing throughout. Some breezy tambourine sounds also pervade the track. As with the previous song, there is another very abrupt ending after the three-minute mark.

'Dirty Deal' (Pop, Williamson)
Yet another sprightly, up-tempo rocker, Iggy takes aim at the music business here as he laments wryly about bad record deals and admonishes record companies:

> Met a creep who gets things done
> He told me I'd be number one
> He knew I was innocent
> I knew he was fucking bent

Meanwhile, James Williamson continues to impress with his Stones-esque guitar sounds. His mid-song licks are a real treat and he also delivers a nice, albeit brief, solo towards the end of the track.

'Beat That Guy' (Pop, Williamson)
A slower-paced number, this penultimate tune features some rather interesting instrumentation and melodic changes. The first half of the song sees James delivering some delicate acoustic guitar sounds, whilst special guests Scott Thurston and Petra Haden add flavour to the proceedings,

respectively, on keyboards and ethereal backing vocals. The last minute of the track then finds James switching to electric guitar, whereby he proceeds to perform a terrific solo. All in all, there is a nice, subtle, melancholic vibe to this tune, with a suitably world-weary vocal turn from Iggy. The more reflective lyrical content finds Iggy dolefully informing us:

> I'm runnin' out of space
> I've run out of time
> I'm runnin' out of reasons
> Though I don't know why

'The Departed' (Pop, Williamson, Asheton)

This closing number, a contemplation on mortality, is also effectively a tribute to past member Ron Asheton. The song begins with a brief, understated, acoustic-based version of Ron's 'I Wanna Be Your Dog' riff before Iggy's almost-spoken croon starts up. Slow and melancholic, this is a moving closing number which features nice, subtle performances from all band members and guest musicians. Of note, guest musician Don Rooke treats us to some lovely electric lap steel sounds, lending a nice country ambience to the piece. Indeed, one is reminded of Johnny Cash and his more sorrowful, later-period output. The track ends with another brief and subtle acoustic-based tease of the 'I Wanna Be Your Dog' riff from James – a fitting tribute to Ron.

Incidentally, an instrumental version of this track was included on the Japanese release of the album as a bonus track.

Other Contemporary Songs
'Dying Breed' (Pop, Williamson)

A slightly pedestrian guitar and drum instrumental opening introduces this album bonus track, which is, ultimately, a little bit of an unremarkable rocker. It is still perfectly listenable and features some recognisably solid, workmanlike drumming from Scott and some Stones-esque lead guitar sounds from James. Iggy, meanwhile, half-heartedly regales listeners with an account of a stray dog's life, which could be taken literally or as an analogy to his own life. Unfortunately, it is all just a little meh and certainly did not merit a slot on the main album.

This track only appeared as a Japanese edition and iTunes edition bonus track.

'3 Stooges' (Pop, Asheton, Asheton)

This was reportedly the final song written by Ron Asheton (together with Iggy Pop and Scott Asheton) and it appears during the credits of the 2012 comedy film *The Three Stooges*. A raucous cacophony of a song with minimal finesse, the trio probably had a lot of fun recording this sub-two-minute throwaway tune. Scott hammers away relentlessly at his drum kit throughout,

Ron's guitar licks squeal and squawk, whilst Iggy throws in a slightly deranged vocal that mainly repeats the song's title. Disposable fun.

Further Related And Recommended Albums And Songs

Metallic KO (1976)

Originally released in 1976 via the Skydog label, the tracks on this legendary live album were purported to be from the band's last ever (at that time) gig at the Michigan Palace (Detroit) in February 1974. However, they were, in fact, from two different gigs at the aforementioned venue. The two gigs in question were dated 6 October 1973 and 9 February 1974 (which was the actual last band gig at that time). The original release contained the Pop/Williamson-penned tunes 'Raw Power', 'Head On', 'Gimme Danger', 'Rich Bitch', 'Cock In My Pocket' and a cover tune, the rhythm and blues/rock and roll standard 'Louie Louie' (Berry). Aside from Iggy, James Williamson, Ron and Scott Asheton, the lineup here also included Scott Thurston on piano.

In 1988, Skydog issued *Metallic 2x KO*, an expanded version of the album which included the following tracks: 'Raw Power', 'Head On', 'Gimme Danger', 'Search And Destroy', 'Heavy Liquid'/'I Wanna Be Your Dog', 'Open Up And Bleed', 'I Got Nothing'/'I Got Shit', 'Rich Bitch', 'Cock In My Pocket' and 'Louie Louie' (again, all penned by Iggy and James except for 'Louie Louie').

The UK-based Jungle Records issued another further expanded set (as a two-disc release) in 1999 (simply entitled *Metallic KO* again), this time with all the tracks correctly assigned to their respective performance dates. Therefore, disc one contains the tracks 'Heavy Liquid' (a fairly new song at the time carried over from 1973 shows), 'I Got Nothin'' (another relatively new song at the time), 'Rich Bitch'/'Baby, Where Did Our Love Go?' (another fairly new number at the time), 'Gimme Danger', 'Cock In My Pocket' (another post-*Raw Power* composition) and 'Louie Louie' from the actual last ever Iggy and The Stooges show (at the time) at the Michigan Palace (Detroit) on 9 February 1974. The second disc contains the tracks 'Raw Power', 'Head On', 'Gimme Danger', 'Search And Destroy', 'Heavy Liquid'/'I Wanna Be Your Dog' and 'Open Up And Bleed' (another post-*Raw Power* song) from the 6 October 1973 gig at the Michigan Palace.

Regarding the newer compositions (at the time), 'Heavy Liquid' is a highly energetic and ebullient piano-driven rock number. This relentlessly paced tune made for a great live track and was performed live during 1973/74. 'I Got Nothin'' is a mid-tempo, Stones-esque rocker with an appealing melody. This thoroughly decent tune was actually recorded a short while later by Iggy and James for their *Kill City* project (detailed later). 'Rich Bitch' is another piano and guitar-driven rocker. However, this up-tempo and exuberant tune does feature some rather crass lyrical content, which lets it down somewhat. Live performances of this song around the time usually ran close to the ten-minute mark. 'Cock In My Pocket' is another piano-driven rock 'n' roller, high on energy and relentlessly paced. It's similar in feel to 'Heavy Liquid' but with more salacious lyrical content (the studio rehearsal version is discussed

Above: Looking mean, moody, tough and defiant, the original lineup of Iggy, Ron, Scott and Dave prepare to take on the world. (*Glen Craig*)

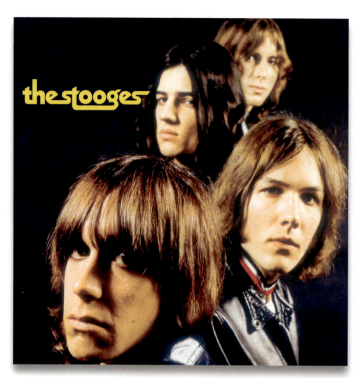

Left: The eponymous debut album, *The Stooges*, exploded onto the scene in 1969. Things would never be the same again… (*Elektra Records*)

Right: The Stooges' legendary sophomore effort, *Fun House*, with a cover hinting at the hellish musical inferno contained within. (*Elektra Records*)

Right: The band take some time to chill out during the recording of *Fun House*. (*Elektra Records*)

Below: Iggy and the band prepare to unleash *Raw Power* onto an unsuspecting world! (*Columbia Records*)

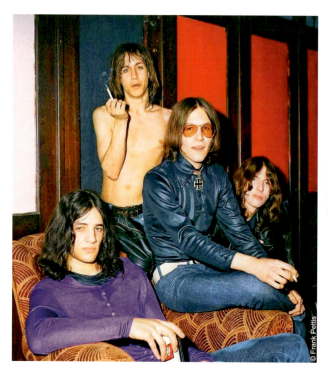

Left: The Stooges enjoy a quick cigarette break circa 1969/70. (*Frank Pettis*)

Right: Backstage at Hollywood's Whisky A Go-Go, 1973. (L-R) Sitting: Iggy, Scott Asheton. Standing: Scott Thurston, Ron, James. (*Richard Creamer*)

Above: The Stooges prowl the stage ominously in their 1970 prime. (*Tom Copi*)

Below: Iggy walks gloriously across the crowd at the Cincinnati Pop Festival in 1970. (*Tom Copi*)

Left: Iggy, Ron and Scott found themselves finally reunited in 2003 on Iggy's *Skull Ring* album. (*Virgin*)

Right: The band's rather disappointing and less than stellar 2007 comeback record, *The Weirdness*. (*Virgin*)

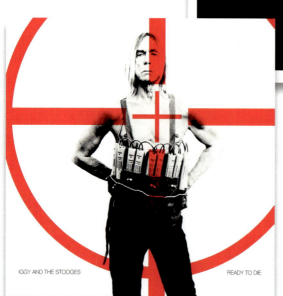

Left: Iggy and The Stooges are *Ready To Die* on their 2013 swan song LP. (*Fat Possum Records*)

Right: Iggy, down and out, on the cover of the legendary live album *Metallic KO*. (*Skydog*)

Left: Iggy and James unleashed *Kill City* in 1977, offering soul-exposing insights into the dark side of mid-1970s LA life. (*BOMP!*)

Right: Celebrating the release of Fun House, the band *Have Some Fun: Live At Ungano's*. (*Rhino*)

Left: Iggy, here in his 60s, still mesmerising audiences with his unique showmanship.

Right: Even when performing in later years, Iggy has continued to be both uncompromising and confrontational.

Left: A triumphant and vindicated Iggy salutes the audience at the 2010 Rock and Roll Hall of Fame induction ceremony.

later). 'Open Up And Bleed', meanwhile, is a slower tempo song, bluesy at times and darkly atmospheric. With passionate vocals delivering a more thoughtful and introspective lyric throughout, this tune is quietly epic (again, the studio rehearsal version is discussed later).

There is some critical feeling that the later expanded editions, whilst being welcome and more historically accurate, nonetheless dilute the power of the original release. I would say that whichever release you pick up, you will be more than happy! This album is, of course, famous for the sound of drink bottles (and various other projectiles) being thrown and smashed at the band on stage! However, despite the audience hostility (and a drug-addled band on the verge of total collapse), the band's musicianship still holds up pretty well!

Metallic KO also proved to be a very influential album on the burgeoning punk scene when it was released in 1976, with the likes of Brian James, Ian Curtis, Peter Hook, John Lydon, Glen Matlock and Joe Strummer all being heavily influenced by the record.

Kill City (1977)

This album, credited to Iggy Pop and James Williamson, is definitely worth a mention, too. This was recorded circa 1975 after the disbandment of The Stooges by Iggy (on weekend release from a psychiatric unit, as detailed earlier) and James. These tracks also feature former Stooge Scott Thurston on keyboards (and bass on some tracks), and there is also further instrumental help from a few other friends.

The original demos were recorded in the hope of attracting a record deal, but no record label interest was forthcoming at the time. However, in 1977, in the wake of Iggy's successful solo albums, *The Idiot* and *Lust For Life*, Bomp! finally released it, albeit remixed and overdubbed in places (incidentally, it was issued in the UK via Radar Records). A newly remixed version (by James Williamson) was also released in 2010 via Alive Naturalsound Records/Bomp!

The eleven tracks, whilst depicting the dark side of mid-1970s LA, actually proffer a more mature, thoughtful and sophisticated listening experience when compared with the Stooges' previous *Raw Power* record. However, where it may lack the fiery and punky aggression of that record, it does offer an appealingly dark and soul-exposing collection of songs wrapped up in a mid-tempo rock ambience.

Catchy at times and soulful at other times, this Stones-soaked ensemble of songs features some terrific vocals from Iggy throughout despite his well-reported mental and physical health issues at the time of recording. He is also on fire lyrically on this record, evincing a dark, biting savagery throughout the album. James Williamson's sterling guitar work and tasty licks throughout also enhance the record greatly. Alongside Williamson's very appealing guitar sounds, the record proffers a variety of musical textures and dynamics as well as an attractive variety of instrumentation throughout (in addition to the standard guitars and drums, listeners are treated to prominent sax sounds, colourful percussion, characterful backing vocals/handclaps, harmonica, etc.).

Two of the album's tracks had actually been performed live during 1973-74 by the James Williamson-era Stooges – 'Johanna' and 'I Got Nothin'' – and they stand out as particular highlights on the record. The sax-soaked former features an irresistible riff from James, fiery vocals from Iggy and some great piano licks courtesy of Scott Thurston. The latter track boasts an intense and emotional vocal from Iggy (counterbalanced by some soothing background 'Oooo's) and a searing mid-song solo from James.

Other highlights include 'Kill City', where Iggy regales listeners with a dark, chilling lyric about the dangers of city living, where you could 'wind up in some bathroom, overdosed and on your knees'. James, meanwhile, produces a fine, swaggering riff on the album's title track. 'Sell Your Love' is a slower, dark ballad which benefits from a bluesy saxophone display and gorgeous soulful backing vocals. 'Beyond The Law', another rocker, features more soulful sax work, albeit used slightly more sparingly, whilst Iggy produces a full-throated vocal in the outro as he informs listeners that 'the real scene is out beyond the law'. 'No Sense Of Crime' is another deliciously dark ballad featuring some pretty bleak lyrics ('Drugs and death are our place in time'), some Ian Stewart (Rolling Stones)-style piano licks and some rather unexpected conga beats.

In conclusion, it is no surprise that the album was generally well-received by critics, both then and now. This is highly recommended listening.

Heavy Liquid (2005/2017)

Throughout the late 1980s and early 1990s, the Revenge label issued loads of live material and compilations containing tracks from the 1972-74 period. In the 1990s to early 2000s, the Bomp! label seemingly took over in terms of releasing material from similar periods (unreleased/live/demo/rehearsal recordings, etc., mainly under *The Iguana Chronicles* series banner).

From the mid-2000s onwards, Easy Action Records took over the unofficial mantle of championing archival Stooges material with numerous live/studio/rehearsal releases. 2005 saw them release the excellent *Heavy Liquid* box set – a six-disc set chronicling the 1972-74 *Raw Power* and beyond era (in terms of demo/rehearsal/live material). 2017 saw Easy Action issue (in single CD/two-LP formats) the same-titled *Heavy Liquid* release, which effectively serves as an alternate/successor album to *Raw Power*, containing, as it does, highlights (from the earlier same-titled box set) of the studio demo and rehearsal tracks from 1972-73. Tracks not already discussed earlier (and composed by Iggy Pop and James Williamson) include:

'Johanna'

Lively at times and moodier-sounding at other times, this guitar and piano-driven number also features a raucous vocal turn from Iggy. It is a full-blooded and thoroughly decent-sounding rocker that showed a lot of potential and promise, even in this rough rehearsal state. It is no surprise that Iggy and James Williamson revisited and recorded this dark tune (possibly about one of Iggy's girlfriends) properly a short while later for their *Kill City* album project.

'Rubber Legs'
Another guitar/piano-driven rocker, this up-tempo and high-energy tune features yet another fully committed vocal performance from Iggy. Not quite as appealing as 'Johanna', this track nonetheless still displayed plenty of potential had it been recorded properly for a possible future album with enthusiastic band performances all around. [Note: This song is sometimes also known as 'How It Hurts'.]

'Open Up And Bleed'
Slower-paced and impressively moody-sounding, this number boasts a terrific soul-exposing vocal display from Iggy. The supporting band instrumentation impresses throughout, too. Overall, it's an understated epic!

'Pinpoint Eyes'/'Cry For Me'
A jaunty barroom rock 'n' roll vibe pervades this mid-tempo track. Driven by honky-tonk piano, this number also features some nice, attractive, bluesy guitar sounds. As with 'Open Up And Bleed', this characterful tune demonstrates more musical sophistication than some of the band's other no-nonsense rock output of the time.

'Cock In My Pocket'
We're back to up-tempo/high-energy rocker territory with this next piano and guitar-driven number. It is a buoyant tune featuring fully committed band member performances. However, although fun and lively, it does suffer a little from some rather crass lyrical content (no surprise, given the song's title)!

'Wild Love'
A mid-tempo, guitar-driven rocker, this one features yet another fully dedicated and full-blooded Iggy vocal turn. The melody's a little lacking though, and in general, the songwriting on display here is a little weaker than other tunes from around this period. However, James' guitar soloing mid-song still impresses. [Note: This song is also sometimes known as 'My Girl Hates My Heroin' and 'Emotional Problems'.]

'Till The End Of The Night' (sometimes "Til The End Of The Night')
A slower-paced number and more moody-sounding, this tune also features a nice haunting melody. Iggy croons, growls, shouts and wails his way through this near-seven-minute epic whilst the rest of the band serve up a suitably

understated instrumental backdrop (until the last minute when the group let rip a bit more, bringing the song to a climax). This is certainly another number that would have had a lot of potential had it been cut in a studio proper for an actual album. [Note: This track is sometimes also known as 'I Got A Problem'.]

Easy Action have issued plenty of other releases pertaining to the Stooges 1972-74 period, but they have also released material dedicated to other years (as well as plenty of Iggy Pop solo material). Other Easy Action Stooges release recommendations include:

You Don't Want My Name, You Want My Action (2009)
This historically important four-CD set contains four shows from the spring 1971 tour, featuring the short-lived, attacking twin-guitar lineup of both Ron Asheton and James Williamson (with Jimmy Recca on bass). At this juncture, the band were playing mostly new songs, of which only 'I Got A Right' would be worked on further in the studio in 1972 (around the *Raw Power* period – see earlier details). Each show contains the same six-song core repertoire. Other songs aside from 'I Got A Right', which was discussed earlier, include the following (and were all penned by Iggy Pop):

'You Don't Want My Name' is a compelling and engaging rock and roll tune and it's a real shame that no studio version was ever cut, as it showed plenty of promise. 'Fresh Rag' is another up-tempo and vibrant rocker featuring enthusiastic band performances. 'Dead Body' (or 'Over My Dead Body')/'Who Do You Love' finds more sizzling and attacking twin guitar sounds dominating. Again, it is a real shame that this particular lineup of the band never got into a studio proper at the time to record some of these numbers. 'Big Time Bum' is a wild, frenzied rock 'n' roll tune driven by more frenetic guitar noise. Again, it is enticing and exhilarating stuff. 'Do You Want My Love?', a fast-paced and high energy-fuelled rocker, finds further thrilling and electrifying guitar sounds dominating the proceedings.

The above tracks are probably some of the songs that Elektra heard, whereupon they then turned around and said 'no thanks' to a third album!

A Thousand Lights (2010)
This contains various 1970 live recordings from when the band were promoting the *Fun House* album.

Theatre Of Cruelty (2022)
A four-CD set featuring four different 1973 shows live at the Whisky A Go-Go.

2020/21 saw Cherry Red enter the fray with two great box set releases that compile a lot of the live/demo/rehearsal material from 1972-74 (*You Think You're Bad, Man? The Road Tapes '73 – '74* and *Born In A Trailer – The*

Session & Rehearsal Tapes '72 – '73). With nine discs in total, these two sets represent a pretty comprehensive overview of that 1972-74 period when the band slowly but surely staggered towards total collapse. It's highly recommended listening.

The Cleopatra label has also issued several compilations over the years (since 1999), usually containing the same bunch of studio demo/rehearsal tracks from 1972/73. However, some of their releases have caused consternation amongst online fandom with suspicions of modern overdubbing!

Other tunes worthy of mention (again, composed by Iggy Pop and James Williamson unless otherwise stated) from this circa 1973 (post-*Raw Power*) period that were recorded in studio rehearsals and never released at the time (but since issued on various subsequent releases from the likes of Easy Action, Cherry Red and Cleopatra) include:

'She Creatures Of The Hollywood Hills' (Pop, Asheton)
This keyboard/guitar-driven rocker is, melody-wise, pretty unremarkable, but the musicianship on display is pretty funky throughout.

'Jesus Loves The Stooges'
A piano-based, ballad-style number, this one emits a subtle but appealing gospel vibe with Iggy crooning and drawling in a suitably guttural fashion throughout. It is okay, but it isn't mind-blowing. This track was actually released as a B-side to an Iggy Pop/James Williamson single issued in 1977 via Bomp! The A-sides were two tracks from their *Kill City* album ('Consolation Prizes' and 'Johanna'). [Note: an instrumental version is also in circulation.]

'Born In A Trailer' (aka 'I Come From Nowhere' and 'Nowhere')
An epic, Stones-esque rocker, this is clearly autobiographical in nature. This thoroughly decent tune runs at just over six minutes in length.

'Hey Baby'
Another keyboard and guitar-driven rocker, this one is distinctly average, with nothing particularly memorable to note.

'Mellow Down Easy' (Dixon)
This is a lively instrumental cover version of the old Willie Dixon tune played at a much faster tempo. The lead guitar is much more to the fore in this version and the drumming is a lot more aggressive. Sadly, there's no harmonica action in this Stooges adaptation, which is a highlight of the original.

'Ballad Of Hollis Brown' (Dylan)
A couple of different band versions of this Bob Dylan cover exist. Firstly, a near-eight-minute rendering featuring guitar and drum machine, which

closely follows the tempo and stark ambience of the original. Iggy plays a little loose with the original lyrics (although it's hard to tell what he's singing sometimes as the audio quality isn't all that great) but it's a decent effort overall.

The second adaptation, around six minutes in length, is played at a faster tempo and features full-band instrumentation, including some great Ray Manzarek-sounding keyboard work, which drives the number along very nicely. Unfortunately, the vocals on this version are also a little obscured due to the poor audio quality, which means the storytelling aspect of the song is spoiled somewhat. Regardless, it is certainly interesting to hear the band tackle Dylan and imbue the song with their own distinctive vibe.

'I'm So Glad' (James)

The band tackle another cover version here, this time Skip James' old blues tune, most famously covered by Cream back in 1966. The Stooges proceed to deliver their own idiosyncratic take on the song at a tempo that's more in keeping with the 1931 original rather than the more frantic Cream version. Indeed, the band also echo the restrained verse/energetic chorus setup of the original, albeit in a far more musically muscular fashion. Overall, it's all a little loose and casual-sounding.

There is some feeling within fandom that the new songs from 1973 are over-reliant on old 1950s rock 'n' roll tropes (even if they are punked up a bit) and are simply not as innovative as previous material. Another common complaint is also the possible overuse of prominent piano in these songs. I guess these criticisms have some merit, to a certain degree, but I do think that amongst the surfeit of post-*Raw Power* material, there are gems to be found, such as 'Open Up And Bleed'.

In addition to the plethora of releases containing this 1972-74 material, there are also other highly recommended releases out there for Stooges fans which cover other material, including the following:

Have Some Fun: Live At Ungano's (Rhino Handmade, 2010)
This August 1970 gig proffers an incredibly forceful and intense performance from the band whilst they were promoting the *Fun House* album.

Sadistic Summer Live 2011 (Concert Live, 2011)
Recorded live at the Isle of Wight Festival, this is a decent gig from the reconstituted James Williamson lineup.

Collection (Australian Tour Edition) (Warner Music Australia, 2011)
This is a two-disc set containing tracks from the first three albums on disc one and some live/alternate versions on disc two.

Gimme Danger (Music From The Motion Picture) (Rhino Handmade, 2017)
This is a nice single-disc Stooges sampler with a few rarities thrown in for good measure.

From KO To Chaos (Skydog, 2020)
A seven-CD + DVD set including all the Stooges/Iggy Pop solo material released by Skydog up to that time. The Stooges stuff includes the original 1976 *Metallic KO* album, the *2x KO* material and *Telluric Chaos* – a live album featuring a terrific March 2004 Tokyo gig by the then recently reformed Stooges.

Live At Goose Lake, August 8th, 1970 (Third Man Records, 2020)
This is a soundboard recording of this historic concert, which proved to be Dave Alexander's last performance with the band. Like most Stooges live recordings, the sound is not necessarily that great, but as a historical document, it is utterly invaluable. This is the infamous final original lineup performance at the Goose Lake Park International Music Festival, where the band were promoting *Fun House*. As mentioned previously, bassist Dave was fired immediately after the gig due to his poor performance. Iggy also apparently took some bad drugs before the gig and was also in a bad way. However, despite all these issues, the band's performance is still great!

The Many Faces Of Iggy Pop (Music Brokers, 2017)
A cheap and cheerful three-CD collection that is worth checking out for its third disc, which contains ten exclusive live tracks from the then recently reformed Stooges (circa 2003) in addition to the ubiquitous 1972/73 demo/rehearsal tracks 'Gimme Some Skin', 'Tight Pants', 'I Got A Right' and 'Raw Power'. Discs one and two contain some nice alternate/live/acoustic/demo recordings from Iggy's solo career.

There are also a couple of general Iggy Pop compilations out there worth mentioning. The 1996 single CD Virgin release *Nude & Rude: The Best Of Iggy Pop* features a smattering of Stooges numbers amongst Iggy's solo hits. More substantial is the two-disc 2005 Virgin release *A Million In Prizes: The Anthology*, which contains a healthier dose of Stooges numbers amongst all the solo tunes.

There are also several Stooges DVDs worth checking out: *Live In Detroit* (the 2003 homecoming reunion gig), *Raw Power Live – In The Hands Of The Fans* (a 2010 concert film from the All Tomorrow's Parties Festival), *Gimme Danger – The Story Of The Stooges* (a film by Jim Jarmusch), *Escaped Maniacs* (a gig recorded at The Lokerse Feesten, Belgium, on 6 August 2005) and also *Tribute To Ron Asheton* (the tribute concert from April 2011 held at Ann Arbor's Michigan Theatre, featuring Iggy and The Stooges, plus special guests Henry Rollins and Deniz Tek).

Epilogue

Sadly, Scott Asheton passed away in March 2014 (from a heart attack, aged 64), followed by the death of Stooge saxophonist Steve Mackay in October 2015. This sadly brought about the end of The Stooges, with James Williamson confirming this officially in 2016:

> The Stooges are over. Basically, everybody's dead except Iggy and I. So, it would be sort of ludicrous to try and tour as Iggy and The Stooges when there's only one Stooge in the band and then you have side guys. That doesn't make any sense to me.

Iggy has continued to act and release new music. James Williamson has also carried on working in the music biz, releasing various solo stuff, including, most notably, the album *Re-Licked*. Released in 2014 via Leopard Lady Records, *Re-Licked* consists of re-workings of unreleased Stooges songs, mostly written by Iggy and James around the *Raw Power* era, with vocals performed by a number of special guests.

2016 also saw the release of the Jim Jarmusch-directed Stooges documentary film *Gimme Danger*, which was very well-received.

And there we have it ... the story of The Stooges. Their legacy has been forever etched into the annals of rock 'n' roll history, and quite rightly, too, for they are a band that spawned countless rock music genres and influenced so many other bands and artists.

Iggy Pop, as a performer, has always been raw, frenzied, unpredictable, intense and primal (the superlatives are endless!), whilst as a lyricist, the man himself knew from the off that he was no Bob Dylan, but he was a master of the improvised lyric made up on the spot. He was, and is, a true original and one-of-a-kind performer!

However, Iggy was not alone in making The Stooges the magnificent beast it was. Ron Asheton, James Williamson, Scott Asheton, Dave Alexander and others all certainly played their invaluable part in establishing the band's legacy. The Stooges were way ahead of their time, and although validation only came much later, they are now rightfully viewed as one of the most important rock bands that ever existed.

I would now like to end proceedings with a few pertinent quotes about the band. From Alice Cooper in the 2005 *The Stooges* reissue liner notes:

> The only band Alice Cooper never wanted to follow was The Stooges ... If we were on a bill with the MC5, The Stooges and The Who, I'd say, 'Can we go on before The Stooges?' As a performer, that's the highest compliment I can pay.

From Jim Jarmusch in the 2017 liner notes to *Gimme Danger – Music From The Motion Picture*:

No other band in rock 'n' roll history has rivalled The Stooges' combination of heavy primal throb, spiked psychedelia, blues-a-billy grind, complete with succinct angst-ridden lyrics and a snarling, preening leopard of a frontman who somehow embodies Nijinsky, Bruce Lee, Harpo Marx and Arthur Rimbaud. There is no precedent for The Stooges, while those inspired by them are now legion. Over the past decades, their influence has bled its way into the culture. Whether in fashion, fine art, or film, the effect of The Stooges remains undeniable.

From author Mike Edison in the liner notes to the 2010 Collectors' Edition reissue of the band's debut album:

The Stooges' influence is legion – to name all of the bands, singers and would-be rock stars who drank from the well could fill 1000 phone books ... There is not a hard or heavy band anywhere on the planet that's not in earnest awe of The Stooges.

Bibliography

Books
Trynka, P., *Iggy Pop – Open Up And Bleed* (Sphere, 2007; reprinted 2008, 2009)
Gold, J., *Total Chaos: The Story Of The Stooges – As Told By Iggy Pop* (Third Man Books, 2016)
Morgan, J., *Iggy And The Stooges – The Authorized Biography* (New Haven Publishing, 2024)
Callwood, B., *The Stooges: Head On: A Journey Through The Michigan Underground* (Music Press, 2016)

Online References
www.discogs.com
www.45cat.com
www.stoogesforum.forumotion.com
www.allmusic.com
www.stoogesdetroit.wordpress.com
www.concerts.fandom.com/wiki/Stooges

DVDs
Iggy & The Stooges – Live In Detroit (Music Video Distributors, Inc., 2004)
Iggy & The Stooges – Escaped Maniacs (ABC Entertainment GmbH/Charly Films LLC, 2007)
Gimme Danger – The Story Of The Stooges (A film by Jim Jarmusch) (Dogwoof Ltd., 2016)
Jesus?.. This Is Iggy (Arte France, 2002)

CD Liner Notes
Fields, D., *The Stooges* (Elektra, 1995)
Edmonds, B., *The Stooges* (Elektra/Rhino, 2005)
Edison, M., *The Stooges* (Elektra/Rhino Handmade, 2010)
Trynka, P., *Fun House* (Elektra/Rhino, 2005)
Levy, A., *Raw Power* (Columbia/Legacy, 1997) – interview with Iggy Pop conducted and edited by Arthur Levy
Needs, K., Bowe, B.J., *Raw Power* (Columbia/Legacy, 2010)

Also available from Sonicbond

On Track series
AC/DC – Chris Sutton 978-1-78952-307-2
Allman Brothers Band – Andrew Wild 978-1-78952-252-5
Tori Amos – Lisa Torem 978-1-78952-142-9
Aphex Twin – Beau Waddell 978-1-78952-267-9
Asia – Peter Braidis 978-1-78952-099-6
Badfinger – Robert Day-Webb 978-1-878952-176-4
Barclay James Harvest – Keith and Monica Domone 978-1-78952-067-5
Beck – Arthur Lizie 978-1-78952-258-7
The Beat, General Public, Fine Young Cannibals – Steve Parry 978-1-78952-274-7
The Beatles 1962-1996 – Alberto Bravin and Andrew Wild 978-1-78952-355-3
The Beatles Solo 1969-1980 – Andrew Wild 978-1-78952-030-9
Blue Oyster Cult – Jacob Holm-Lupo 978-1-78952-007-1
Blur – Matt Bishop 978-178952-164-1
Marc Bolan and T.Rex – Peter Gallagher 978-1-78952-124-5
David Bowie 1964 to 1982 – Carl Ewens 978-1-78952-324-9
David Bowie 1963 to 2016 – Don Klees 978-1-78952-351-5
Kate Bush – Bill Thomas 978-1-78952-097-2
The Byrds – Andy McArthur 978-1-78952-280-8
Camel – Hamish Kuzminski 978-1-78952-040-8
Captain Beefheart – Opher Goodwin 978-1-78952-235-8
Caravan – Andy Boot 978-1-78952-127-6
Cardiacs – Eric Benac 978-1-78952-131-3
Wendy Carlos – Mark Marrington 978-1-78952-331-7
The Carpenters – Paul Tornbohm 978-1-78952-301-0
Nick Cave and The Bad Seeds – Dominic Sanderson 978-1-78952-240-2
Eric Clapton Solo – Andrew Wild 978-1-78952-141-2
The Clash (revised edition) – Nick Assirati 978-1-78952-325-6
Elvis Costello and The Attractions – Georg Purvis 978-1-78952-129-0
Crosby, Stills and Nash – Andrew Wild 978-1-78952-039-2
Creedence Clearwater Revival – Tony Thompson 978-1-78952-237-2
Crowded House – Jon Magidsohn 978-1-78952-292-1
The Damned – Morgan Brown 978-1-78952-136-8
David Bowie 1964 to 1982 – Carl Ewens 978-1-78952-324-9
David Bowie 1964 to 1982 – Carl Ewens 978-1-78952-324-9
Deep Purple and Rainbow 1968-79 – Steve Pilkington 978-1-78952-002-6
Deep Purple from 1984 – Phil Kafcaloudes 978-1-78952-354-6
Depeche Mode – Brian J. Robb 978-1-78952-277-8
Dire Straits – Andrew Wild 978-1-78952-044-6
The Divine Comedy – Alan Draper 978-1-78952-308-9
The Doors – Tony Thompson 978-1-78952-137-5
Dream Theater – Jordan Blum 978-1-78952-050-7
Bob Dylan 1962-1970 – Opher Goodwin 978-1-78952-275-2
Eagles – John Van der Kiste 978-1-78952-260-0
Earth, Wind and Fire – Bud Wilkins 978-1-78952-272-3
Electric Light Orchestra – Barry Delve 978-1-78952-152-8
Emerson Lake and Palmer – Mike Goode 978-1-78952-000-2
Fairport Convention – Kevan Furbank 978-1-78952-051-4

Also available from Sonicbond

Peter Gabriel – Graeme Scarfe 978-1-78952-138-2
Genesis – Stuart MacFarlane 978-1-78952-005-7
Gentle Giant – Gary Steel 978-1-78952-058-3
Gong – Kevan Furbank 978-1-78952-082-8
Green Day – William E. Spevack 978-1-78952-261-7
Steve Hackett – Geoffrey Feakes 978-1-78952-098-9
Hall and Oates – Ian Abrahams 978-1-78952-167-2
Peter Hammill – Richard Rees Jones 978-1-78952-163-4
Roy Harper – Opher Goodwin 978-1-78952-130-6
Hawkwind (new edition) – Duncan Harris 978-1-78952-290-7
Jimi Hendrix – Emma Stott 978-1-78952-175-7
The Hollies – Andrew Darlington 978-1-78952-159-7
Horslips – Richard James 978-1-78952-263-1
The Human League and The Sheffield Scene – Andrew Darlington 978-1-78952-186-3
Humble Pie –Robert Day-Webb 978-1-78952-2761
Ian Hunter – G. Mick Smith 978-1-78952-304-1
The Incredible String Band – Tim Moon 978-1-78952-107-8
INXS – Manny Grillo 978-1-78952-302-7
Iron Maiden – Steve Pilkington 978-1-78952-061-3
Joe Jackson – Richard James 978-1-78952-189-4
The Jam – Stan Jeffries 978-1-78952-299-0
Jefferson Airplane – Richard Butterworth 978-1-78952-143-6
Jethro Tull – Jordan Blum 978-1-78952-016-3
J. Geils Band – James Romag 978-1-78952-332-4
Elton John in the 1970s – Peter Kearns 978-1-78952-034-7
Billy Joel – Lisa Torem 978-1-78952-183-2
Journey – Doug Thornton 978-1-78952-337-9
Judas Priest – John Tucker 978-1-78952-018-7
Kansas – Kevin Cummings 978-1-78952-057-6
Killing Joke – Nic Ransome 978-1-78952-273-0
The Kinks – Martin Hutchinson 978-1-78952-172-6
Korn – Matt Karpe 978-1-78952-153-5
Led Zeppelin – Steve Pilkington 978-1-78952-151-1
Level 42 – Matt Philips 978-1-78952-102-3
Little Feat – Georg Purvis – 978-1-78952-168-9
Magnum – Matthew Taylor – 978-1-78952-286-0
Aimee Mann – Jez Rowden 978-1-78952-036-1
Ralph McTell – Paul O. Jenkins 978-1-78952-294-5
Metallica – Barry Wood 978-1-78952-269-3
Joni Mitchell – Peter Kearns 978-1-78952-081-1
The Moody Blues – Geoffrey Feakes 978-1-78952-042-2
Motorhead – Duncan Harris 978-1-78952-173-3
Nektar – Scott Meze – 978-1-78952-257-0
New Order – Dennis Remmer – 978-1-78952-249-5
Nightwish – Simon McMurdo – 978-1-78952-270-9
Nirvana – William E. Spevack 978-1-78952-318-8
Laura Nyro – Philip Ward 978-1-78952-182-5
Oasis – Andrew Rooney 978-1-78952-300-3

Also available from Sonicbond

Phil Ochs – Opher Goodwin 978-1-78952-326-3
Mike Oldfield – Ryan Yard 978-1-78952-060-6
Opeth – Jordan Blum 978-1-78-952-166-5
Pearl Jam – Ben L. Connor 978-1-78952-188-7
Tom Petty – Richard James 978-1-78952-128-3
Pink Floyd – Richard Butterworth 978-1-78952-242-6
The Police – Pete Braidis 978-1-78952-158-0
Porcupine Tree (Revised Edition) – Nick Holmes 978-1-78952-346-1
Procol Harum – Scott Meze 978-1-78952-315-7
Queen – Andrew Wild 978-1-78952-003-3
Radiohead – William Allen 978-1-78952-149-8
Gerry Rafferty – John Van der Kiste 978-1-78952-349-2
Rancid – Paul Matts 978-1-78952-187-0
Lou Reed 1972-1986 – Ethan Roy 978-1-78952-283-9
Renaissance – David Detmer 978-1-78952-062-0
REO Speedwagon – Jim Romag 978-1-78952-262-4
The Rolling Stones 1963-80 – Steve Pilkington 978-1-78952-017-0
Linda Ronstadt 1969-1989 – Daryl O. Lawrence 987-1-78952-293-8
Roxy Music – Michael Kulikowski 978-1-78952-335-5
Rush 1973 to 1982 – Richard James 978-1-78952-338-6
Sensational Alex Harvey Band – Peter Gallagher 978-1-7952-289-1
The Small Faces and The Faces – Andrew Darlington 978-1-78952-316-4
The Smashing Pumpkins – Matt Karpe 978-1-7952-291-4
The Smiths and Morrissey – Tommy Gunnarsson 978-1-78952-140-5
Soft Machine – Scott Meze 978-1078952-271-6
Sparks 1969-1979 – Chris Sutton 978-1-78952-279-2
Spirit – Rev. Keith A. Gordon – 978-1-78952- 248-8
Stackridge – Alan Draper 978-1-78952-232-7
Status Quo the Frantic Four Years – Richard James 978-1-78952-160-3
Steely Dan – Jez Rowden 978-1-78952-043-9
The Stranglers – Martin Hutchinson 978-1-78952-323-2
Talk Talk – Gary Steel 978-1-78952-284-6
Talking Heads – David Starkey 978-178952-353-9
Tears For Fears – Paul Clark – 978-178952-238-9
Thin Lizzy – Graeme Stroud 978-1-78952-064-4
Tool – Matt Karpe 978-1-78952-234-1
Toto – Jacob Holm-Lupo 978-1-78952-019-4
U2 – Eoghan Lyng 978-1-78952-078-1
UFO – Richard James 978-1-78952-073-6
Ultravox – Brian J. Robb 978-1-78952-330-0
Van Der Graaf Generator – Dan Coffey 978-1-78952-031-6
Van Halen – Morgan Brown – 9781-78952-256-3
Suzanne Vega – Lisa Torem 978-1-78952-281-5
Jack White And The White Stripes – Ben L. Connor 978-1-78952-303-4
The Who – Geoffrey Feakes 978-1-78952-076-7
Roy Wood and the Move – James R Turner 978-1-78952-008-8
Yes (new edition) – Stephen Lambe 978-1-78952-282-2
Neil Young 1963 to 1970 – Oper Goodwin 978-1-78952-298-3

Also available from Sonicbond

Frank Zappa 1966 to 1979 – Eric Benac 978-1-78952-033-0
Warren Zevon – Peter Gallagher 978-1-78952-170-2
The Zombies – Emma Stott 978-1-78952-297-6
10CC – Peter Kearns 978-1-78952-054-5

Decades Series
The Bee Gees in the 1960s – Andrew Mon Hughes et al 978-1-78952-148-1
The Bee Gees in the 1970s – Andrew Mon Hughes et al 978-1-78952-179-5
Black Sabbath in the 1970s – Chris Sutton 978-1-78952-171-9
Britpop – Peter Richard Adams and Matt Pooler 978-1-78952-169-6
Phil Collins in the 1980s – Andrew Wild 978-1-78952-185-6
Alice Cooper in the 1970s – Chris Sutton 978-1-78952-104-7
Alice Cooper in the 1980s – Chris Sutton 978-1-78952-259-4
Curved Air in the 1970s – Laura Shenton 978-1-78952-069-9
Donovan in the 1960s – Jeff Fitzgerald 978-1-78952-233-4
Bob Dylan in the 1980s – Don Klees 978-1-78952-157-3
Brian Eno in the 1970s – Gary Parsons 978-1-78952-239-6
Faith No More in the 1990s – Matt Karpe 978-1-78952-250-1
Fleetwood Mac in the 1970s – Andrew Wild 978-1-78952-105-4
Fleetwood Mac in the 1980s – Don Klees 978-178952-254-9
Focus in the 1970s – Stephen Lambe 978-1-78952-079-8
Free and Bad Company in the 1970s – John Van der Kiste 978-1-78952-178-8
Genesis in the 1970s – Bill Thomas 978178952-146-7
George Harrison in the 1970s – Eoghan Lyng 978-1-78952-174-0
Kiss in the 1970s – Peter Gallagher 978-1-78952-246-4
Manfred Mann's Earth Band in the 1970s – John Van der Kiste 978178952-243-3
Marillion in the 1980s – Nathaniel Webb 978-1-78952-065-1
Van Morrison in the 1970s – Peter Childs – 978-1-78952-241-9
Mott the Hoople & Ian Hunter in the 1970s – John Van der Kiste 978-1-78-952-162-7
Pink Floyd In The 1970s – Georg Purvis 978-1-78952-072-9
Suzi Quatro in the 1970s – Darren Johnson 978-1-78952-236-5
Queen in the 1970s – James Griffiths 978-1-78952-265-5
Roxy Music in the 1970s – Dave Thompson 978-1-78952-180-1
Slade in the 1970s – Darren Johnson 978-1-78952-268-6
Status Quo in the 1980s – Greg Harper 978-1-78952-244-0
Tangerine Dream in the 1970s – Stephen Palmer 978-1-78952-161-0
The Sweet in the 1970s – Darren Johnson 978-1-78952-139-9
Uriah Heep in the 1970s – Steve Pilkington 978-1-78952-103-0
Van der Graaf Generator in the 1970s – Steve Pilkington 978-1-78952-245-7
Rick Wakeman in the 1970s – Geoffrey Feakes 978-1-78952-264-8
Yes in the 1980s – Stephen Lambe with David Watkinson 978-1-78952-125-2

Rock Classics Series
90125 by Yes – Stephen Lambe 978-1-78952-329-4
Bat Out Of Hell by Meatloaf – Geoffrey Feakes 978-1-78952-320-1
Bringing It All Back Home by Bob Dylan – Opher Goodwin 978-1-78952-314-0
Californication by Red Hot Chili Peppers - Matt Karpe 978-1-78952-348-5
Crime Of The Century by Supertramp – Steve Pilkington 978-1-78952-327-0

Also available from Sonicbond

The Dreaming by Kate Bush – Peter Kearns 978-1-78952-341-6
Let It Bleed by The Rolling Stones – John Van der Kiste 978-1-78952-309-6
Pawn Hearts by Van Der Graaf Generator – Paolo Carnelli 978-1-78952-357-7
Purple Rain by Prince – Matt Karpe 978-1-78952-322-5
The White Album by The Beatles – Opher Goodwin 978-1-78952-333-1

On Screen Series
Carry On... – Stephen Lambe 978-1-78952-004-0
David Cronenberg – Patrick Chapman 978-1-78952-071-2
Doctor Who: The David Tennant Years – Jamie Hailstone 978-1-78952-066-8
James Bond – Andrew Wild 978-1-78952-010-1
Monty Python – Steve Pilkington 978-1-78952-047-7
Seinfeld Seasons 1 to 5 – Stephen Lambe 978-1-78952-012-5

Other Books
1967: A Year In Psychedelic Rock 978-1-78952-155-9
1970: A Year In Rock – John Van der Kiste 978-1-78952-147-4
1972: The Year Progressive Rock Ruled The World – Kevan Furbank 978-1-78952-288-4
1973: The Golden Year of Progressive Rock 978-1-78952-165-8
Eric Clapton Sessions – Andrew Wild 978-1-78952-177-1
Dark Horse Records – Aaron Badgley 978-1-78952-287-7
Derek Taylor: For Your Radioactive Children – Andrew Darlington 978-1-78952-038-5
Ghosts – Journeys To Post-Pop – Matthew Restall 978-1-78952-334-8
The Golden Age of Easy Listening – Derek Taylor 978-1-78952-285-3
The Golden Road: The Recording History of The Grateful Dead – John Kilbride 978-1-78952-156-6
Hoggin' The Page – Groudhogs The Classic Years – Martyn Hanson 978-1-78952-343-0
Iggy and The Stooges On Stage 1967-1974 – Per Nilsen 978-1-78952-101-6
Jon Anderson and the Warriors – the Road to Yes – David Watkinson 978-1-78952-059-0
Magic: The David Paton Story – David Paton 978-1-78952-266-2
Misty: The Music of Johnny Mathis – Jakob Baekgaard 978-1-78952-247-1
Musical Guide To Red By King Crimson – Andrew Keeling 978-1-78952-321-8
Nu Metal: A Definitive Guide – Matt Karpe 978-1-78952-063-7
Philip Lynott – Renegade – Alan Byrne 978-1-78952-339-3
Remembering Live Aid – Andrew Wild 978-1-78952-328-7
Thank You For The Days - Fans Of The Kinks Share 60 Years of Stories – Ed. Chris Kocher 978-1-78952-342-3
The Sonicbond On Track Sampler – 978-1-78952-190-0
The Sonicbond Progressive Rock Sampler (Ebook only) – 978-1-78952-056-9
Tommy Bolin: In and Out of Deep Purple – Laura Shenton 978-1-78952-070-5
Maximum Darkness – Deke Leonard 978-1-78952-048-4
The Twang Dynasty – Deke Leonard 978-1-78952-049-1

Would you like to write for Sonicbond Publishing?

We are mainly a music publisher, but we also occasionally publish in other genres including film and television. At Sonicbond Publishing we are always on the look-out for authors, particularly for our two main series, On Track and Decades.

Mixing fact with in depth analysis, the On Track series examines the entire recorded work of a particular musical artist or group. All genres are considered from easy listening and jazz to 60s soul to 90s pop, via rock and metal.

The Decades series singles out a particular decade in an artist or group's history and focuses on that decade in more detail than may be allowed in the On Track series.

While professional writing experience would, of course, be an advantage, the most important qualification is to have real enthusiasm and knowledge of your subject. First-time authors are welcomed, but the ability to write well in English is essential.

Sonicbond Publishing has distribution throughout Europe and North America, and all our books are also published in E-book form. Authors will be paid a royalty based on sales of their book. Further details about our books are available from www.sonicbondpublishing.com. To contact us, complete the contact form there or email info@sonicbondpublishing.co.uk